The Wildlife of Shropshire

CONTENTS

Acknowledgements

The photographs in this book are the result of eighteen years sporadic and accumulated work. Over this time literally dozens of people have helped in countless ways and it is embarrassing to admit that I cannot remember all of them. However amongst the many who have assisted I would like to say a particular thank you to Adrian Bayley, Ian Dean-Netscher, Dave Fulton, Jonathan Hodges, Julian Langford, Rachel Lees, John Neilson, Keith Offord, Nick Pinder, Colin Powell, Matti Selanne, Ian Scott, David Woodfall and Colin Wright. I would like to add a special note of thanks to Marilyn Dixon and John Dickens at Pentax U.K. for help with their superb camera equipment. Finally I would like to thank my wife Judith for help, advice and tolerance of the strange goings-on that inevitably accompany wildlife studies.

About the Author

Michael Leach has been a wildlife photographer and author since 1977. He has written eight other books on subjects ranging from great apes to owls, and his pictures have been used in more than 500 books in a total of 40 countries. Michael travels widely in search of wildlife subjects and in recent years has worked with polar bears in the Arctic, orang-utans in Borneo and sperm whales around the Azores. He has been fascinated by Shropshire's wildlife since an early introduction on nature walks from Buildwas Junior School at the age of seven.

Michael and his wife Judith live, with their two children, in Kinnerley near Oswestry.

Introduction

Wildflower meadow

Introduction

Shropshire does not have towering mountains or rugged coast-lines; it has no National Parks or giant waterfalls; neither does it have crowded cities, a high population or heavily polluted skies. The biggest single problem facing wildlife in this country is loss of habitat. As cities expand they encroach upon more of the countryside; fields and woodlands are gradually being replaced by housing estates and roads. The one priceless resource that Shropshire can offer is clean and uncrowded space.

With its small human population and large area, Shropshire is astonishingly fortunate. Compared to many other regions, this county is relatively underdeveloped and even the cultivated land is not as intensively farmed as it could be. As a result wildlife is still diverse and abundant, if you know where to look for it.

This book is not only a guide to finding and identifying Shropshire wildlife, it also tells the story of why the animals live here and how they fit into their specific environment. The book is divided into chapters covering the different habitats found in the county, and looks at the animals that live within them.

Some species are not confined to one single habitat; foxes can be seen trotting over the Long Mynd and also crossing over busy main roads in Telford. These and a few other adaptable animals have been included in the environments where they are most likely to be seen. Due to the restrictions of space, not every Shropshire species is covered. We have chosen those that are most likely to be seen or are particularly interesting.

Where possible old local terms have been included. These were used for wild animals long before the modern 'standard' lists came into force. Some date back many centuries and even within one county there were often many different names for one single animal. Some were wonderfully poetic while others verged on the insulting. The goldfinch was known in Shropshire both as the 'lady with seven flounces' and 'spotted dick'.
It is not only the names that have altered,

the fortunes of the wildlife itself have constantly changed for a variety of reasons. Some species prosper while others suffer. In 1281 Edward I employed a hunter by the name of Peter Corbet 'to take and destroy all the wolves he can find in ... Shropshire'. In the past fifty years we may have lost the corncrake and woodlark as breeding species but we have gained collared doves and Canada geese, birds that would have been seen as truly exotic in the 19th century. It was not too long

ago that the red squirrel was a common animal; these have now gone and in their place we have the grey squirrels. A healthy eco-system is never static, but unfortunately many of the recent changes have been man-made rather than natural.

Shropshire is a privileged county and, on a personal level, I would like to add that it is special to me. I have worked with exciting wildlife all over the world but there is a unique thrill to watching the ways of the animals that share my home landscape. Some of my most treasured wildlife experiences have taken place within walking distance of my office. Few moments can match the time a kingfisher sat on a low branch of our apple tree and preened for several minutes before disappearing through the leaves in a turquoise blur.

The book is divided into habitats not just for ease of identification: Much has been written about bio-diversity over recent years and for good reason. Many of the world's wild animals have evolved for life in a specific environment; if that disappears then the animals that live there will also vanish. The concern for bio-diversity is based around a need to maintain and protect all habitats, in order that the wildlife that relies upon them for food and shelter may survive. Overhunting may not

be a major problem in Shropshire today, but the threat of habitat destruction is real and this can be just as lethal as putting a bullet through the heads of the animals that live there.

Shropshire wildlife is an asset to be enjoyed but it also needs to be protected and safeguarded. I do not want to be part of the last generation that can walk the wild hills and forests; we must bequeath the same right and pleasure to our grandchildren and their descendants. To give them that experience in the future we must take care of what we have – today.

Michael Leach.
Kinnerley
December 1996

Opposite, top: Wolves were found in Shropshire until about the middle of the 14th century.

Opposite, bottom: Red squirrel.

Above: Grazing land provides an excellent feeding ground for wild birds.

Woodlands

Woodlands

Woodlands, as we know them today, appeared around 15,000 years ago at the end of the last great Ice Age. Birch and aspen were probably the first trees to creep up from the warm south and take root in the bleak wilderness left by the retreating ice-sheets. Hazel, pine, oak and elm soon followed. Eventually almost the whole country was covered with thick forest. Shropshire was one huge woodland. Today 99% of Britain's forest has disappeared and it is humans that are to blame. Man first arrived here about six thousand years ago and from the very beginning exploited the woodlands. Forests supplied fuel for fires, timber for buildings and wooden tools for hunting. Settlements were often found on the highest ground of the forest, such as the hill forts at Nesscliffe and Clee Hill. A high position was easier to defend, and was often drier and less overgrown. Neolithic forests were probably nothing like the gentle woodlands we see today. They were totally wild and unmanaged, dense and difficult to walk through. In the forest lived wolves, lynx and bears – all of which were found in Shropshire.

*Commercial fir plantations provide
a much narrower range of food and breeding
opportunities than can be found in native
deciduous woodlands*

As agricultural skills developed more
land was cleared to make way for crops,
the growing number of farm animals also
had an effect as they grazed through the
forest. By the time of the Domesday Book
survey of 1086, we can see that Britain had
already lost much of its original tree cover.
At that time the human population of
Shropshire was probably around 15,000
at the most, and as only about 20% of the
county was forested, this gives us an idea
of just how much timber had already been
used by a small number of people.

As early as the 11th century it was
realised that forests were an asset to
be treasured and guarded. The original
meaning of the word forest was 'an area
set aside for hunting'. The best hunting
was in woodland and the two terms soon
became interchangeable. Cnut was the first
King to see the threat to the habitat and
he introduced some tough laws to prevent
the forests being overhunted. Edward the
Confessor later created a small army of
wardens to keep away poachers. For centuries
access to the best forests was allowed only
to a select few; these were the first private
hunting estates. Most woodlands were
protected by fences and ditches to deter
poaching and the theft of timber.
The woodlands on and around the Wrekin
are the remnants of a much larger hunting
forest that was known as Mount St Gilberts.
Wild boar and deer thrived here. Many of the
venison joints that appeared on the banqueting
table of Henry III came from Shropshire.

There was another surge in the rate of forest
destruction in the Middle Ages brought about
by the need for good strong building wood.
Britain was developing into a major power
and its population was growing rapidly.
Oak trees were in demand as the solid
backbone of the countless timber-framed
houses which sprang up in the 15th, 16th
and 17th centuries. An average of three
hundred trees were used to make a single
house and oak was always the first choice.
Strangely enough one of the most destructive
periods took place during this century.
As the human population mushroomed
and Britain's post war economy slumped,
it became increasingly important to produce
more of our own food. Over the past fifty
years countless trees have been felled to
make way for increasingly large and viable
agricultural fields.

In wildlife terms, a mature forest is quite
simply one of the most complex and
important habitats on earth. It is estimated
that 90% of the world's land animals have
specifically evolved for life in the forest.
Woodlands provide shelter, breeding sites
and an astonishing variety of food for an
equally remarkable diversity of animals.
The food chain starts in a small way:
Insects feed on hundreds of different
woodland plant species. Birds and mammals
eat the insects, together with nuts and
berries. Deer browse on new leaf growth
while worms feed on those leaves that fall
to the ground. Butterflies flit out of view at
tree-top level, while wood mice live beneath
their roots.

The loss of our old forests is one of the greatest disasters ever to happen to British wildlife. Shropshire fortunately has more woodland than most counties and, as a result, we have the chance to see more of the specialist wildlife that lives there.

Badgers

The striped face of the badger is one of the most distinctive sights in British wildlife. The tell-tale mask is a warning to allcomers that this is a potentially dangerous animal and should be avoided. Badgers are powerful, growing up to a metre long, and weighing 16kg. In addition to the familiar black-and-white animals, Shropshire also has albino badgers and a rare strain known as 'erythristic', where the animals are a strange ginger colour.

For centuries the country name for the badger was 'brock' and the setts in which these animals lived were so large and important that they became local landmarks. The Shropshire village names of Brockton and Brockhurst are derived from the badgers that lived there. They are nocturnal animals that rarely stir before dusk. Spending their days underground, they sleep in one of the many tunnels and dens that make up a badger sett. These may have been used by countless generations of badgers and can be several hundred years old, each containing dozens of dens and entrance holes. In Shropshire some setts are so deep that the badgers dig up coal when extending the tunnels.

The most important part of a badger's diet is the humble earthworm. But they are true omnivores and will eat almost anything they find, such as mice, slugs, hedgehogs, apples, and a long list of other items. Badgers are closely related to otters, stoats and weasels; they live in family groups ranging from two to thirty individuals of all ages.

Badger cubs are born underground in early spring. The usual litter size is two or three, and they will not emerge from their den until around eight weeks old. Badgers can live up to fifteen years in the wild. They have no natural predators in this country. The biggest threat to badgers is road traffic and, sadly, baiters that kill the animals for their own perverted pleasure.

Muntjac

The muntjac is a strange little animal that must have made many people doubt their senses. About the size of a small dog, just 43cm (17in) high, this secretive deer is a rare but fascinating addition to Shropshire wildlife. There are two species of muntjac in Britain, the Indian and Chinese, but only aficionados can tell the two apart, and they can interbreed. Muntjac arrived here at the end of the 19th century. The first escapes took place from Woburn Abbey in

Bedfordshire. As the deer bred their range slowly increased but no-one is sure exactly when they first arrived in Shropshire, simply because they are so very difficult to see.

Although the muntjac is a true deer, it does not fit the standard 'Bambi' image. Males have long canine teeth in their top jaw which protrude down over their lower lip and bear a strong resemblance to small tusks. Muntjac do have antlers but they are thin, weak affairs that are used mainly for show. Tusks are used for serious fighting, and not just amongst themselves. They have a great dislike of dogs and, instead of running away, will often stand and fight when threatened by an animal much larger than themselves.

To add to the surreal illusion, muntjac have a very un-deer-like call that sounds exactly like a yapping terrier. Unless the deer is visible, most listeners will swear that the sound is made by a dog. Muntjac eat grass and leaves all year round, and in the autumn they fatten

up on acorns and apples in preparation for the winter ahead. They live in mixed grassland or woodland, staying anywhere that offers thick cover. These animals are active mainly at night; their days are passed sleeping in thick vegetation, hidden from the eyes of all that pass by.

Muntjac go to great lengths to avoid humans, even though they may live close by. Few people ever suspect the presence of a miniature deer with tusks, that barks like a dog and eats acorns, but the species is now part of the Shropshire fauna. At the moment they are confined to the east and south but their range is expanding. Muntjac are too big to be threatened by native British predators and no-one bothers hunting them, so their future in the county looks quite rosy.

Yellow-Necked Mouse

Few observers would notice the difference between a wood mouse and a yellow-necked mouse, but they are two entirely different species. As the name suggests the latter has a yellow collar which circles the neck. Unfortunately, as these animals are nocturnal and painfully wary of humans, this is very difficult to see. And even in adults the collar can be a wishy-washy colour or not properly formed.

Size is a good indicator of yellow-necked mice, as they are much bigger and heavier than wood mice. In fact they exceed wood mice in almost every department; they are much more likely to bite when handled; they enter houses more often and are far noisier.

Wood mice only squeak in moments of excitement or stress, and normally the sound level is so low that it goes unnoticed by humans. The yellow-necked mouse, on the other hand, is a very noisy creature which can be heard by anyone without a severe hearing problem. But jumping is the yellow-necked mouse's most impressive ability.

Leaping is an effective way of avoiding predators and few British mammals can match the long-jumping skills of a yellow-necked mouse. From a standing start they can leap almost three feet in one bound.

The species is found throughout Shropshire; in fact the county is one of its national strongholds. Anyone seeing this animal tends to dismiss it as a wood mouse, which is a pity as this is a species not found in too many other areas. The two species are related and share similar habitats, but the yellow-necked mouse is less likely to venture into open areas away from the shelter of woods and hedges. They can live up to two years in the wild.

Wood Mouse

After rats and humans, wood mice are the most numerous mammals in Shropshire. Their name indicates that they belong in forests, which is perfectly true, but they also live in many other habitats. Wood mice are nocturnal animals that spend the daylight hours sleeping in underground tunnels. The only visible clue to their presence is a small hole, the size of a ten pence piece, tucked away beneath a hedge or bush. Wood mice can be identified by their long tails and huge ears. The ears serve an important function. They act as collecting dishes which pick up the slightest sound that may be made by a stalking cat or weasel.

In the cloak of darkness an acute sense of hearing is far more important than eyesight, and as a rule nocturnal animals generally have bigger ears than their diurnal cousins.

At dusk wood mice venture out to look for food. Their diet is varied and interesting, ranging from nuts and fruit to fungi and caterpillars. In the bleak winter months, when natural food becomes scarce, wood mice have been known to enter houses. The standard technique for breaching security is simply to climb up the outside wall and get into the attic under the eaves. At home I have several peanut feeders attached to windows with powerful suckers; almost every night wood mice climb the vertical surface of the window frame and jump over to the feeder. There they sit for up to an hour, gorging themselves on the protein rich nuts before simply dropping off and disappearing into the night. They are superb acrobats and climbers; wood mice are, for their size, among the most powerful jumpers in Britain.

Dormouse

The 'seven-sleeper' is a wonderfully accurate name for this small animal as it passes over half of every year in hibernation. The dormouse spends just five months, May to September, awake; the other seven months are spent sleeping in a den made of leaves and grass, hence the name. Dormice were once common throughout Shropshire. Victorian naturalists tell us that they could be found in most copses. Like so many other species, the dormouse is now depressingly rare.

Shropshire dormice are found mainly in, and around, the Clun Forest in the south-west of the county. As seed eaters they are very partial to woodland and hedgerows for these are the best places to find nuts;

Opposite, top: Wood mouse.
Opposite, bottom: Dormouse.

hazel, sweet chestnut and beech are eagerly eaten. They particularly like coppiced woodland, where trees are regularly trimmed by foresters to produce long poles and good strong growth. But coppicing is quickly becoming a dying art and this prime dormouse habitat is slowly vanishing.

Dormice are completely nocturnal and the only real way to find them is to search the tree-tops and hedges with a powerful torch. Their eyes reflect like mirrors and a lucky observer may notice two tiny red-glowing pinpricks staring back through the branches. That is usually the end of the encounter – dormice may appear slow and clumsy in daylight but at night they are fast and incredibly agile. A dormouse threatened by a human will simply leap unpredictably into the undergrowth, to be swallowed up by the darkness. The only wild dormice I have seen were discovered entirely by accident. All were asleep inside birds' nest-boxes, which make warm and safe daynests for a sleepy dormouse.

Grey Squirrel

There is no mention of this species in the classic work "Fauna of Shropshire". When it was published in 1899 grey squirrels were rare here while their cousins the red squirrel were "found all over the county, wherever there are woods."

Grey squirrels were originally a North American species. The first ever known sighting of the animal in Britain was just across the border from Shropshire at Llandisilio Hall in 1828, and soon afterwards at Llanfair Caereinion. No-one knows where these animals came from as the earliest recorded introduction did not take place until 1876, when a pair was released in Cheshire. At first they were seen as an exciting new animal and many more were imported and released, including a large number near Wrexham in 1903.

Shropshire is a good example of our ambivalent attitude to grey squirrels. In rural areas, they are seen as highly destructive pests that strip trees of their bark and damage valuable forestry plantations. While in towns they are valued as entertaining visitors to the garden. The behaviour of urban squirrels is very different to that of their rural counterparts. In country areas, grey squirrels avoid humans at all costs, as close contact often results in a shotgun blast. In towns however the squirrels can become so tame that they feed directly from a human hand. In Telford, there are several people who have trained squirrels to enter their homes to take food.

They may be cute and cuddly but there is little doubt that grey squirrels are a damaging addition to Shropshire's wildlife. To add to their diet of seeds and nuts, they raid birds' nests to eat eggs and chicks, and their presence will always deter the return of red squirrels.

The grey squirrels thrived in their new habitat. They bred so rapidly that in 1938 it became illegal to release any new specimens into the wild. Everyone knows the story from this point: Grey squirrels went on to colonise almost the whole of England and Wales, and parts of lowland Scotland. Today the Welsh Marches are listed as containing one of the grey squirrels' highest populations. Grey squirrels are not quite the villains of popular myth. One widespread theory is that, because they are larger and more aggressive, grey squirrels drove out the native red squirrels and occupied their territory. Most zoologists reject this, as red squirrels were already declining before their American cousins arrived, due to a viral disease that had affected most of the population. When the grey squirrels appeared there were large tracts of squirrel-free woodlands and they could simply move in. But it is fair to say that once the grey squirrels took up residence, the red squirrels had no chance of winning back their territory.

Whiskered Bat

Whiskered bats are one of the smallest of their family in Britain and they are extremely hard to identify, even for experts. Academic books tell us that whiskered bats are unusually hairy, and have black noses and ears. But as these animals are normally seen only as flittering silhouettes against a fading sky, these tips are of little help.

The bats are permanent residents in Shropshire and their population is probably low. But as there are so few people with the skill to recognise them, it is impossible to know the true story. Whiskered bats are usually found feeding near woodland, although they prefer to roost and hibernate in caves and roof spaces. They often fly along hedgerows collecting airborne insects attracted by night-flowering plants. Any small bat seen purposefully following a hedge-line is probably a whiskered bat. To solve the problem it is possible to use a gadget known as a bat detector. This listens to the high-pitched call made by bats and lowers the frequency to a level that can be heard by humans. Each species of bat gives out different calls. Detectors are extremely useful when trying to recognise flying bats.

Whiskered bats are experts at snatching food directly from trees and are very partial to eating spiders. With pinpoint accuracy a flying bat spots a spider on a twig and, with a deft twist of its wing, performs a half roll and picks up the unsuspecting victim with razor sharp teeth. It is a wonderful performance to watch.

Long-Eared Owl

To the first time viewer long-eared owls are surprisingly small, only about two thirds the size of a tawny owl. The owl's name is very misleading for the distinctive 'ears' have nothing to do with hearing, they are simply tufts of long feathers that help the bird's camouflage. The real ears are narrow slits on either side of the head, hidden deep beneath the feathers.

Long-eared owls are now uncommon in Shropshire, with a population as low as thirty breeding pairs. These are widely scattered throughout the county, generally well away from built-up areas. Strangely, long-eared owls on mainland Europe live mainly in deciduous forests, while here they show more of a preference for conifer woodlands. The long-eared is the only British

owl that roosts in colonies; when territories overlap, several owls can be found sleeping in the same tree. Long-eared owls have a very curious call, sounding just like someone blowing over the neck of a half-filled milk bottle. Many people must have heard the noise without ever knowing what they were listening to.

Long-eareds lay their eggs in nests made and abandoned by other birds. Crows' nests are the first choice. Some Shropshire ornithologists are now experimenting with artificial nest sites in the form of wire platforms, securely attached to branches, in an effort to attract more owls.

Tawny Owl

The old Shropshire name for this bird is 'billy hooter', coined because of the owl's persistent, echoing call. The evocative "kee-witt" of the tawny owl is the outstanding nocturnal sound of Shropshire woodlands, particularly in autumn when the birds are fighting over territorial rights. A dusk walk through the woods of the Wrekin, Wenlock Edge or around the Clun Forest is usually rewarded with the haunting call of a tawny that is noisily announcing its hunting rights before setting out in search of food.

Although tawny owls prefer deciduous forests, they are highly adaptable birds capable of

Above: A tawny owl's long legs are usually hidden amongst thick feathers, they are only visible when the owl stretches them down to land or kill.

living in almost any habitat, including towns. The total population of the county is around fifteen hundred breeding pairs, at least thirty-five of which live within the Telford boundary. The reason for the owls' success is their wide ranging diet; they will eat anything from earthworms up to young rabbits and almost everything in between. Frogs, mice, the occasional bat and even other owls are taken when the chance arises.

Tawnies, like other owls, do not build elaborate nests, instead they breed inside hollow trees. They have also been known to lay their eggs in rabbit warrens when suitable trees are scarce. Tawny owls will happily take to artificial nest boxes and this is one of the most effective methods of attracting a breeding pair. Female tawny owls are larger and heavier than their mates and the two generally form a pair bond that lasts for life.

Green Woodpecker

This bird's maniacal, laughing call is echoed in the old Shropshire name of 'yawkle'. For such a retiring species they have collected a surprising number of local names: 'high hoe', 'laughing bird', 'rain-pie' and 'eaqual' have all been used. The name 'rain-pie' refers to the woodpecker's supposed ability to summon rain. Eighteenth century stories tell us that farmers knew when rain was due when they heard woodpeckers call.

These are the largest of Britain's woodpeckers and are widely distributed throughout Shropshire, with a population which may be as high as one thousand pairs.

Green woodpeckers are far less likely to be seen than the more numerous and bolder great spotted woodpecker. The green woodpecker's name is a little misleading as their wood-pecking is mainly restricted to nest building. Green woodpeckers feed on ants which they collect on the ground. They usually nest on the edge of a woodland or amongst scattered trees but are often seen in open areas such as golf courses and parkland where they use their beaks and long tongues to probe the turf looking for food.

Great Spotted Woodpecker

The great spotted is the most visible of Shropshire's three woodpeckers and, with a population of around 2,500 pairs, it is also the most common. They can be found anywhere that offers a selection of mature trees; young plantations are of no use at all. Great spotted woodpeckers feed on the larvae of wood boring beetles which burrow in the softening trunks of dead or dying trees.

Great spotted woodpeckers do sometimes live in oak woodlands, but it is not a perfect habitat for them. Oak trees have a long life span, up to six hundred years, and it takes many centuries for them to become soft enough for a woodpecker to drill easily and longer still before they rot sufficiently to allow the excavation of nesting holes. These woodpeckers prefer trees with a shorter life cycle. Silver birch are perfect, they begin to die back at around sixty years old. In any stand of birch, there should always be a fair number that are soft enough for a woodpecker's probing beak.

Top, right: Green woodpecker.
Bottom, right: Great spotted woodpecker.

The nest of great spotted woodpeckers is built high up in the tree trunk about three and a half metres (12ft) above the ground. The hole is bored by both male and female, using their long, powerful beaks. The chamber is unlined and five or six white eggs are laid directly onto the small chips of wood left by the hole-drilling. Great spotted woodpeckers produce the noisiest chicks I have ever heard, they keep up an incessant chattering which can be heard a long way from their hidden nest.

Until recently they were exclusively woodland birds but, like so many other species, woodpeckers suffer in winter and many die through the twin effects of cold and hunger. In cold weather many great spotted woodpeckers venture out of the forest, and will cross fields and roads to reach a well-stocked bird-table. They will take almost any food, but are particularly keen on peanuts and lard.

Bullfinch

The old English name for the bullfinch was 'alpe', from this came one of its Shropshire names of 'nope'. There are two other recorded local names: 'black nob' from the bird's black head and 'lum budder' from its habit of nipping off fruit buds. Bullfinches are not always popular with gardeners because of their habit of eating fresh new buds on apple and plum trees. Male and female often feed together and are efficient workers. A pair will move onto a newly budding tree and systematically strip it in a matter of hours. Fortunately bullfinches do not rely entirely on fruit trees and will eat a wide variety of seeds and nuts.

Bullfinches are found all over the county, avoiding only high ground and very open landscapes where food is hard to find. They often move into gardens during winter, feeding together in small flocks. In spring

Opposite: Bullfinch

they nest in thick hedges and bushes. Over recent years in Shropshire bullfinches have shown a slow but noticeable shift towards nesting in gardens, which may be because more people are leaving out food on bird-tables and the bullfinches are learning to take advantage. When the breeding season comes, they simply stay close to their new feeding area.

Hawfinch

In the high tree-tops lives the shy and chunky hawfinch. For its size, the hawfinch has one of the most impressive beaks of any species. In fact the whole bird looks robust and tough. But few people get to admire its physique as hawfinches hardly ever venture down to ground level.

In Shropshire the hawfinch, together with the chaffinch, is known as a 'piefinch', which is probably a reference to the black and white (or pied) feathers in its plumage. The modern name comes from the fact that they like to eat hawthorn berries. This is certainly true, but cherries are really their favourite food. Their large, powerful beaks can easily crack open a cherry stone; a feat that would be beyond the jaws of many humans. The scientific name of the hawfinch is *coccothraustes*, which comes from the Greek term for nut-cracker. They also eat yew berries, a food that can be fatal to humans.

Hawfinches are very rare in Shropshire. There is only a small resident breeding population which does not seem to be increasing. They are creatures of the woodland, who prefer mature trees in mixed or deciduous forests. Their usual habitat suggests that they should be found in the south of the county, where there are more trees. But hawfinches can be seen almost anywhere in Shropshire, even though sightings may be fleeting and infrequent. During the winter months hawfinches often leave their breeding territories and join up with others to form feeding flocks. These have been seen frequently in the forest at Whitcliffe near Ludlow.

Sparrowhawk

In the 1960s the sparrowhawk population in Shropshire was in dire trouble. The over-use of chemical pesticides and a widespread campaign against them by gamekeepers had a terrible effect. They became so rare that they were included on Schedule One of the Protected Birds Act which lists those species that are in the greatest need of legal protection. Today the situation has completely turned around. Sparrowhawks are thriving with a population of around fifteen hundred breeding pairs.

The birds themselves are very shy and elusive. Most sightings occur when the hawk's attention is taken up with hunting. Sparrowhawks eat small birds and usually catch them in mid-air; once suitable prey is chosen a sparrowhawk will chase it for some distance. With a swift and acrobatic flight the hawk relies on astonishing manoeuvrability and speed to overtake small birds, and, during the chase, it is oblivious to everything. Once, at Selattyn near Oswestry, a sparrowhawk actually hit my head as it chased a panic-stricken great tit along a hedgerow.

Opposite: Sparrowhawk.

Like all hawks, the female sparrowhawk is larger and more powerful than the male and therefore tends to take bigger prey; a female is capable of catching a bird as large as a wood pigeon, while males specialise in song birds. The difference in size avoids conflict over food between the pair during the nesting season.

Sparrowhawks are well distributed throughout the county but increasingly they are being seen around gardens where householders feed birds. Sparrowhawks feed off bird-tables, not eating nuts and seed, but the birds themselves. In winter months bird tables provide the best chance of seeing sparrowhawks. They have learned to sit and wait on chimney pots or television aerials until a suitable meal appears. Sparrowhawks are particularly keen on human habitation on the edge of towns, close to nearby woodlands. They are free to hunt birds in domestic gardens while still nesting in the secrecy of a high tree-top further out in the countryside. Gardens on the edge of Bridgnorth and Ludlow are excellent places for aspiring sparrowhawk watchers.

Nuthatch

'Nutcracker' is the Shropshire name for the nuthatch, and it is well chosen. Nuthatches enjoy eating acorns and hazel nuts, but they are tough and not easily opened by small birds. So the wily nuthatch jams the nuts into a crevice in a tree and hammers away with its powerful beak, the bird uses its whole body weight against the nut and quickly cracks the hard shell.

In Shropshire nuthatches are becoming increasingly reliant on bird tables in winter, particularly in March and April, when the nuts and seeds from the previous winter have all been eaten and the new crop has yet to appear. The scarcity of food through these two months brings about the highest mortality in wild birds, even though the worst of the cold weather may be over.

Nuthatches are birds of deciduous woodland, and their county stronghold is in the south, where mature oak forests are at their best. Folklore tells us that nuthatches always go down a tree, rather than up it. They are, in fact, the only British bird that can walk head first down a tree trunk, but they can also walk up it and even move sideways around it. Nuthatches often breed in old woodpecker nesting holes. As woodpeckers are larger than nuthatches, the entrance hole is much bigger than necessary. To reduce the chance of the nest being raided by squirrels or other predators, nuthatches plaster mud around the edge of the entrance hole until it is just big enough to squeeze through.

Rook

Rooks are difficult birds to categorise into habitats; they nest in woodlands but feed in open fields. They are colony breeders that nest very close together, often with as many as ten pairs in a single tree. Rookeries are large, noisy hives of activity that are impossible to miss. Some sites have been used for generations and the nests are simply repaired each year when the birds return to breed.

Rooks and crows have long been confused and this has given us some strange ideas. The humble scarecrow was never really intended to frighten away crows as they are not a major problem to arable farmers. Rooks, on the other hand, love feeding on newly sown seeds and can be a real pest. Mis-identification gave us the name scarecrow which we all know today, but the truth is that the tatty manikins standing in countless Shropshire fields should be called 'scare-rooks'.

It is worth mentioning that although rooks do take seeds they also eat a huge number of invertebrates, such as leather-jackets, that later would do enormous damage to growing crops if they were not eaten themselves. Unfortunately this side of the rooks' feeding is usually overlooked, while it is all too easy to spot where the birds have dug up seeds. As a result rooks are known for their destructive qualities and the good they do goes unnoticed. Rooks are thriving in Shropshire, their population remains stable at around twenty thousand breeding pairs.

Wood Warbler

Not long ago any small insect-eating bird was assumed to be a member of the wren family, which explains the wood warbler's old name of yellow wren. Wood warblers are a member of a group known as the 'leaf-warblers', the other two Shropshire species being willow warbler and chiff-chaff. All three are summer visitors from Africa that arrive in late April and early May. The males are the first to appear and quickly announce territorial rights with a long, piping call, which is impossibly loud for such a small bird. On warm, still spring evenings, the wood warbler's voice is one of the more dominant.

Wood warblers are very choosy about their breeding sites; they will only nest in

Opposite, top: Rook
Opposite, bottom: Wood warbler

'hanging woodland', that is a wood that grows on a steep slope. The trees must be mature, with a thick canopy, and the vegetation on the ground beneath should not be too dense. This bird was photographed on the Wrekin, after a painfully long search. Wood warbler's camouflage their nests so well that they can remain unnoticed even when a human is less than one footstep away.

Garden Warbler

With a name like garden warbler, it would be reasonable to expect these birds to appear in a different chapter. However the garden warbler has been badly named for, although they are occasionally found in gardens, their usual habitat is deciduous woodland. The garden warbler's main claim to fame is its fluent song but, like so many of the bird world's most accomplished singers, this is a physically unremarkable, even drab species.

Unless an observer has a keen ear for birdsong, the garden warbler is likely to go completely unnoticed due to its total lack of distinguishing features. Even the song causes difficulties as a garden warbler sounds horribly like a blackcap to all but a real expert. Garden warblers are migrants that spend their winters in southern Africa and arrive here in late April.

They are secretive insect-eating birds that quietly and unobtrusively search for food under the cover of vegetation, rarely venturing into open areas. Their nests are well hidden in thick foliage and are extremely difficult to find as the adults rarely show themselves even when ferrying food to hungry chicks. Garden warblers are widely distributed throughout Shropshire, and are found in most mature deciduous forests, their highest numbers are in the south and west, and in the woodlands of Wenlock Edge and the Wrekin.

Chiff-Chaff

Along with the cuckoo, this is one of the few birds whose name echoes its call. With the naked eye, or even with the help of binoculars, the three leaf warblers are fiendishly difficult to tell apart. The chiff-chaff is perhaps the easiest to identify because of its unique "chip-chop, chip-chop" call. This is a useful aid because chiff-chaffs and willow warblers are almost the same size with near identical plumage. To make the task even more confusing, the habitat of the three warblers overlaps in many places throughout the county. Sometimes the nature of the breeding territory can help in differentiating the species. Willow warblers will nest almost anywhere with thick vegetation, including scrubland and moorland, whereas chiff-chaffs and wood warblers prefer mature deciduous woodland.

In June chiff-chaffs can be found nesting in almost every reasonably sized, ungrazed wood in Shropshire. All of the leaf warblers are migrants; the chiff-chaff, which spends its winters in central Africa, is the first to arrive and is often seen in Shropshire by the end of March. This is a risky strategy: If all goes well the birds have a strong territorial hold on prime breeding sites before rival migrant species arrive, but if spring is late, or a cold snap strikes, the warblers may find there is nothing to eat.

Redstart

Redstarts are appropriately called 'fiery-brand-tails' in Shropshire, after the rich chestnut-red tail displayed by both males and females. Their modern name comes from 'steort' which is an early Anglo-Saxon word for tail. Another local name is white cap, but this only really refers to the male, whose flamboyant red and black plumage is topped with a white crown. The female is an altogether more subdued colour.

Redstarts are hole-nesters, behaviour which restricts the species to areas containing mature trees. Although in recent years they have taken to breeding in artificial nest boxes, helping to extend their range a little. Redstarts are migrants that arrive here in April and stay until the end of August, when they head for the warm forests of West Africa.

Like most British migrants, redstarts fly south in late summer because their food supply disappears. Insects can be found year round in West Africa, so why do the birds come back here to breed? Most ornithologists believe that migrants return to Britain because it is home to fewer birds and therefore the competition for food and nest sites is reduced.

Redstarts do well in Shropshire woodlands, as the high tree canopy in June and July is crawling with the larvae of saw-flies and moths, and the fly population is at its greatest.

They are active birds that rarely stay still while looking for food; as they have an average of seven chicks in a brood, they need to work hard to keep them all fed. In Shropshire the species is found mainly in the deciduous forests of the south-west and Clun Forest, Corve Dale and the lower reaches of the Long Mynd. All these areas have healthy breeding populations. There are other small pockets dotted around the rest of the county.

Wren

The wren could have been included in any one of the chapters in this book. They are very successful and adaptable birds that thrive in a huge variety of habitats. In Shropshire they are found everywhere from Telford's parks to the rock strewn uplands of the Stiperstones. The wrens' preferred habitat is probably open woodland, but in good years their breeding rate can be so high that their healthy population needs to colonise all possible areas. Like all very small birds they are vulnerable to cold winters. When the temperature falls dramatically wrens often roost together in small cavities to keep warm. In one Much Wenlock nest box 42 wrens were found huddled together on a sub-zero February morning.

Wrens breed in beautiful nests made of moss and grass. They have a small hole in the front that looks like a cave, and from this structure

comes the wren's scientific name of 'troglodytes' – the cave dweller. Wrens can lay up to sixteen eggs in a clutch, but this is only reached when there is an excellent food supply and the adults have a good chance of feeding such a large family. Normally the nest is wedged into a tree fork but they can be found in nesting boxes, inside dry stone walls or hollow trees and under house eaves.

The male wren has a busy mating season because he may build several nests in his territory and install a different female in each. The male shows his mate each of the available nests and she chooses one in which she will lay her eggs. In Shropshire, as in many other areas, there was once a strange ritual that took place on Boxing Day and sometimes lasted until Epiphany. The whole community, but particularly young boys, would set out on a wren hunt. This was a serious business and hundreds of wrens were killed in a single day.

This is a pre-Christian tradition that dates back to the time when the wrens were seen to represent the dying year. The ritual slaughter of the wrens made room for the New Year to begin, bringing with it the all-important promise of warmth and new life. This tradition continued until the turn of the 20th century in parts of Shropshire.

This photograph was taken close to the embankment of the Severn Valley Railway near Highley. Incredible as it may seem a female cuckoo had laid an egg inside the tiny wren's nest. That acrobatic feat alone defies the imagination but worse was to come. As the young cuckoo matured, it outgrew its home and the nest simply disintegrated. The two adult wrens had to work overtime to feed their foster child, who consumed more than four times the food eaten by a whole family of wren chicks.

Goldcrest

The goldcrest is Shropshire's smallest bird, just 9cm (3.5in) long. Their size and tiny weight allow them to search for insects on the very end of thin branches that could not support bigger birds. Although this gives goldcrests an exclusive feeding ground, a diminutive body size does have one massive disadvantage – it loses heat very quickly. In cold weather goldcrests can literally freeze to death because they cool so rapidly. A single cold snap of a week or so can almost wipe out an entire population.

Goldcrests usually nest in conifers, which is why they are so often found in Forestry Commission plantations. The nest is a tiny cup suspended from the end of a branch. It is made of moss, spiders' webs and lichens and is no bigger than a child's clenched fist. Goldcrests compensate for their vulnerability to cold weather by producing an awful lot of chicks. They often lay ten eggs but the number can be as high as thirteen, and they usually have two clutches every spring. Goldcrest numbers may fluctuate but as each pair can produce twenty live offspring every year, the species can soon recover from a bad winter.

Goldcrest numbers in Shropshire can swing dramatically anywhere between 20,000 to 50,000 in a single year. These birds can be found in almost every mixed or coniferous woodland in the county and are one of the very few species that have benefited from the growth of commercial plantations. Foresters have long been criticised for creating sterile vacuums when they plant huge stands of exotic fir trees, but the goldcrest at least has made full use of the new habitat.

Out of the breeding season goldcrests visit gardens far more often than people realise and yet they are hardly ever noticed. As they feed high in the trees, these tiny birds are difficult to spot and, even when they are seen, it is from below, the tell-tale ridge of gold feathers on top of their heads is completely hidden and the bird is often mistaken for something else.

Coal Tit

Along with the goldcrest the coal tit is one of the few Shropshire birds that specialises in conifer woodlands. Their nickname of 'black cap' perfectly fits a bird whose most distinctive feature is a heavy black hood. The word 'coal' is a reference to the black head, but does not come from the fuel that is dug out of the ground. It is an abbreviation of charcoal which is much closer in appearance to the matt black of a coal tit's crown.

Coal tits stay in their woodland home when food is plentiful. Being members of the tit family, they can perform wonderful acrobatics while searching for food, often hanging upside down. They use their sharp beaks to pick out insects that lie hidden in bark crevices or amongst pine needles. They also eat seeds from cones, these are a rich source of protein but are well protected and need a lot of work to collect. Like so many of their relatives, when winter arrives, coal tits frequently move into gardens and rely on bird-tables as their main food supply.

Gardens are purely a temporary solution for coal tits, when spring returns they move back to the woodlands ready for breeding. Nests are built in hollow trees or occasionally holes in old walls. Sometimes they occupy nest boxes, but very few are put up in conifer woodlands due to the low number of birds that breed there. Coal tits are found all over Shropshire, living in even the smallest stands of woodland, only high exposed areas are avoided.

Coal tits are frequently noticed in gardens, but in their forest habitat they are well hidden amongst the foliage and are usually way above the heads of walkers. Few people bother bird-watching in conifer woodlands, as there are too few birds to see. This lack of observers is reflected in the scarcity of sightings, but this can give a false picture because coal tits are one of Shropshire's most numerous birds.

Rivers, Streams & Lakes

River Severn at Bridgnorth

Rivers, Streams & Lakes

In the natural world water means life. It starts off at the microscopic level with tiny plants and single-celled animals floating freely in the water. These are eaten by larger creatures and then they too are eaten by even bigger animals. The pattern continues until at the top of the aquatic food chain in Shropshire we see otters, grey herons and mink.

The great waterway is the River Severn and this has a huge effect on the county's natural history. Not only does the river act as home to many animal species but, along with its tributaries, it drains the land and creates small and important habitats such as mud banks, flood plains and thick bankside vegetation.

We are particularly lucky with the River Severn as it rises in the unpolluted hills of Wales and is still clean and well oxygenated when it flows over the border into Shropshire. The nature of the river changes as it flows east. Around Melverley, where the land is flat and banks are low, the river floods almost every year and creates a silt-rich feeding ground for curlews, herons and other birds. Further east, the banks become steeper as the river carves its path through a more undulating landscape such as the Ironbridge Gorge. Here is a less changeable habitat that is not so prone to flooding as the river is well held by its high banks. These areas have a higher fish population which, in turn, attracts kingfishers and other aquatic predators.

It would be a terrible mistake to see the Severn as the only worthwhile river for wildlife. Smaller tributaries can be even more interesting as they have fewer visitors. The Worfe, Teme and Tern are wonderfully rich habitats that are wilder than many parts of the Severn but are often overlooked. Flowing rivers are not ideal for all aquatic animals, some need the stability of still water and to find these perhaps the best place to start looking is around the meres of north Shropshire.

These lakes form the largest area of open water in the county and were created following the last great ice age around twelve thousand years ago. There are nine meres dotted around the town of Ellesmere, and several less well known examples near both Baschurch and Shrewsbury. They range in size from the Mere in Ellesmere, which measures 114 acres, down to smaller versions such as Kettle Mere and Betton Pool, which are simply large ponds. Some go entirely unnoticed and the best example of this is Weeping Cross Mere which is a stone's throw from the junction of the Shrewsbury by-pass and the A458 Bridgnorth road.

There are many more stretches of open water in Shropshire, some of which are man-made. The pools in Telford Town Park are home to

several species of waterfowl and are useful drinking and roosting areas for birds passing through. But the inevitable human disturbance around urban pools keeps away the more wary animals. The meres are important as many of them are inaccessible to the public, allowing sensitive species to breed and feed without interference.

It is tempting to think that the pools in wilderness areas, like the Shropshire Hills, should contain the richest variety of wildlife but this is far from true. Water on high, exposed land is usually too cold to support much animal life and it often contains high levels of tannin from the peat and surrounding vegetation. This makes it an unsuitable habitat for water insects or plants and without these at the bottom end of the food chain, few larger animals can survive.

Otters

The "Fauna of Shropshire" (1899) notes that "In Shropshire the Otter is found on the Severn and most of the larger streams, and in some parts is numerous". Sadly things have changed dramatically since this was written, now the otter is a rare but welcome sight. In recent times overhunting wiped out every known breeding pair, but today the Shropshire otters' future is looking a little more secure.

Hunting has been banned, landowners and gamekeepers are generally much more sympathetic to the presence of predators and a long-term project has been launched that should give the otters a good chance of re-colonising the county. Captive bred otters have been released into Shropshire, at carefully selected, secret sites which provide both good feeding and breeding grounds.

Re-introduction is a slow and time-consuming business, and success is far from guaranteed. Theoretically, with its network of streams and rivers, and relatively few humans,

Shropshire is a near perfect environment for otters. But newly released otters must master the techniques of hunting, and breed successfully, if they are to provide the nucleus of a thriving population. It will be many years before we see if this project has succeeded. Early signs are encouraging as wild otters have now been spotted inside Shrewsbury itself. A single animal was seen walking across a car park in Frankwell, an event that has probably not been witnessed for several decades.

Mink

One hundred years ago this animal could not have been included in a book on Shropshire wildlife for it had yet to arrive in the country. The mink that now patrols so many of our lakes and rivers is a member of the weasel family, a close relative of stoats, badgers and of course otters. It is also an invader and not even a descendant of the species that lives wild on the European mainland. British mink come originally from North America.

Live mink were first imported to Britain in 1929. They were destined to become breeding stock in commercial fur-farms that were springing up throughout the country. Mink are tough, agile animals and inevitably there were escapes from the moment they first arrived. Regular reports of wild mink appeared shortly after the war. The animals found themselves in an ideal habitat with no direct competition either for food or breeding sites. Otters were already becoming scarce by then and their population was too low and restricted to pose a threat to the burgeoning mink numbers.

Wild mink were first reported in Shropshire in the late 1950s; today they have moved into most of the county's waterways and their numbers are still increasing. In captivity mink are selectively bred in a variety of different, commercially attractive colours, ranging from fawn to jet black and every conceivable hue in between. In the wild, the offspring of escaped animals quickly revert to their natural colour which is a rich chocolate brown, often with a creamy white 'bib' on the chest and throat.

In behaviour and superficial appearance, mink are very similar to otters and they both share a liking for wet habitats. Distant identification can be tricky and many casual observers convince themselves that they have seen an otter rather than a mink. But this is usually wishful thinking as mink are far more numerous. The two animals differ in size: Otters are 1.2m (47in) long and weigh 11kg (24lb), much larger and heavier than the mink which is just 1.8kg (4lb) and 65cm (25in) long.

Small size does not make the mink any less of a hunter. They are skilled and powerful carnivores that eat a huge range of prey animals. Mink are accomplished swimmers and climbers, allowing them to catch fish in the water and raid birds' nests high in the trees. One Shropshire fisherman tells of a mink that stole his keep net and ripped it open to reach the live fish stored inside. The mink did this just three metres away from the watching angler, who was so astonished that he did not

interfere. Mink possess one further advantage, they are not intimidated by the presence of humans, unlike the far more wary otter.

Pipistrelle

The pipistrelle is the smallest and most numerous of our native bats, and they are still a common sight throughout Shropshire even though numbers are falling. This is one of several species known as the water bat because of its habit of hunting over lakes. Pipistrelles are often seen hawking for insects under river bridges in places like Atcham and Bridgnorth. Recently they have taken up residence in some of the small crevices found in the bridges over the Montgomery canal, which has been cleaned and restored and is now a wonderful wildlife habitat. Bats feed over water simply because it attracts large numbers of flying insects. Pipistrelles are not at all confined to water but it is an excellent place to start looking for them. Evening is the best time

to watch as they emerge from day-roosts about half an hour after sunset.

Secure roosts are vitally important for the survival of bats. They are needed for sleeping, hibernating and breeding. Roosts are moved several times a year to compensate for changes in temperature. The careful choice of a breeding site is essential. When space allows, female bats form huge nursery colonies consisting of up to three hundred adults and their young. Males are excluded from these maternity groups and live nearby, alone or with just one or two others. In November pipistrelles must find a hollow tree or building for hibernation. Before turning in for their long winter sleep, each bat must feed quickly and heavily, building up reserves to see them through to the following spring.

Pipistrelles are the only bats that can be seen flying in winter and this confuses some viewers as everyone assumes that the bats' winter sleep is unbroken. But this species does wake up on warm days or if it has used up the last reserves of body fat and needs to go out in search for food. Pipistrelles flying in February have caused many arguments amongst naturalists in the past. Hibernating bats may be inactive but they still use around a quarter of their body weight to keep their temperature high enough to prevent death. This technique obviously works as pipistrelles are a long lived species, with a maximum life span of eight years.

Water Vole

This round, shaggy creature is the immortal 'Ratty' character from Kenneth Grahame's book 'Wind in the Willows', and the flesh-and-blood animal is not dissimilar to its literary counterpart. Water voles' lives are centred around unpolluted rivers, pools and canals. They are surprisingly large and can grow as big as a guinea pig. The species is almost universally known as the water rat, which is a foul slur because water voles are far less intrusive, damaging and disease-ridden than rats.

It is unfortunate that the inoffensive water vole has been lumped together with rats, as this has warped our view of them. They are often seen as pests to be destroyed but the truth is that they are harmless grass-eating vegetarians that never come into buildings and do virtually no damage to crops. The confusion is understandable because brown rats live close to water and swim very well. Superficially the two species are similar but water voles have a much 'chubbier' appearance than a rat, their heads are rounder and their tails shorter. They also lack the rat's obviously huge ears.

Water voles are expert swimmers that are more at home in water than on land. They breed in underground tunnels built close to the water's edge, these also act as bolt-holes where they can hide from predators.

Water vole numbers are declining rapidly in Shropshire. They are having an increasingly hard time because of the growing number of mink in the county. These are now the water voles' major predator, as they often share the same habitat. A change in the management of waterways has also had its effect. Water voles require thick vegetation next to water, this provides both shelter and food. Over the past two decades there has been a growing trend towards keeping banks clear of plants to prevent waterways becoming overgrown. Sometimes the clearance is too severe, leaving no vegetation at all. The water voles then move out, but they do not always find an alternative replacement for their lost habitat.

Canada Goose

The canada goose does not have an old Shropshire name as it has not been here long enough to have been given one. As the name suggests these birds are originally from North America. The first known reference to the species in Britain dates back to the 17th century when they were kept in St James's Park in London as part of a bird collection owned by Charles II. Royal patronage quickly made them very popular exotic additions to the wildfowl displays of stately homes all around the country. They began to escape immediately.

Canada geese were occasional visitors to Shropshire and did not really start to breed here seriously until well into the 20th century, but they are making up for it now. Canada geese build nests very close to water, either pools or rivers, where they stay for the whole of the breeding season. During the rest of the year they fly long distances in search of food, looking particularly for newly harvested fields where they collect cereal seeds missed by the farmers' machines. Canada geese are big birds that eat a large amount of food and their voracious behaviour has lead to calls from some conservationists to control their numbers. There is a strong argument for culling as these powerful geese keep away our native birds from their traditional feeding areas. The county now has a canada goose population estimated at more than two thousand birds, and their numbers are growing.

Second in size only to the mute swan, canada geese are large enough to defend themselves against almost all predators. Only foxes pose a real threat to adults. Wild canada geese will quickly become humanised when free food is on offer. The birds at Ellesmere are totally wild, yet can be hand-fed.

Grey Heron

The herons of Ellesmere are amongst the best known of all Shropshire birds, because they have become a major tourist attraction. Every year an observation post is set up, equipped with telescopes and binoculars, where visitors can watch the intimate happenings of the breeding colony without disturbing the birds. A closed circuit television system has now been added and the scheme has been an outstanding success, attracting several thousand visitors each spring.

Away from Ellesmere, grey herons are far more difficult to watch, they are timid birds with a small population measuring less than 250 birds. Their nests, usually in colonies close

to water, are at the top of very tall trees and are completely inaccessible. The largest and oldest of Shropshire's heronries is at Halston Park near Whittington. Herons are at their most visible as they fly between feeding sites. With their huge wingspan and slow, ponderous flight, they cannot be mistaken for any other bird. When flying the heron's long neck is pulled back into a distinctive 's' shape.

Herons are scattered throughout Shropshire but nowhere can they be described as common. They often hunt in shallow water, searching for fish, eels and frogs, and will also eat small mammals such as voles and mice given the opportunity. Well stocked garden pools are tempting feeding grounds for herons, as they often contain a far higher density of fish than would ever be found in the wild. But as herons are wary, they usually raid ponds shortly after dawn, before the resident humans are around to chase them away.

Kingfisher

Just to make life difficult, the old Shropshire name for the kingfisher is 'dipper', which is a completely different species today. The Greeks knew the bird as Halcyon, and it is this source that we unknowingly quote when speaking of the 'halcyon days of summer', referring to a time when the sun shines and kingfishers are at their brilliant best.

The Fauna of Shropshire (1899) notes that kingfishers are "the most brightly coloured of British Birds, and therefore shot upon every opportunity". Fortunately our habits have changed and now the kingfisher enjoys complete legal protection. But this is not a guarantee of survival as these birds are extremely vulnerable to cold weather. Low temperatures keep fish in deeper water and out of reach and, at its worst,

Opposite: This kingfisher is holding the fish by the tail, a sure sign that the food will be fed to a chick as kingfishers always swallow fish headfirst.

winter seals off the kingfishers' feeding grounds under a thick layer of ice.

It may take many years for the population to recover from a single harsh winter. The numbers for Shropshire fluctuate anywhere between 300 pairs down to almost zero. One problem facing kingfishers in other areas is largely missing here. Severe water pollution reduces the fish population and destroys the kingfishers' food supply. Shropshire's rivers rarely suffer from this, as much of the water runs from the Welsh hills and does not pick up any industrial outflow before it arrives here.

Kingfishers can be seen hunting in any waters where fish are found, they will raid garden ponds and commercial fisheries, and can also be seen along canals and around lakes. But their breeding activity is usually confined to larger rivers, the Severn, Vyrnwy and Clun rivers are all favourite nesting habitats. This bird was photographed on the Rea Brook. Kingfishers build their nests at the end of long tunnels excavated in sandy banks. The only visible sign is a small entrance hole about the size of an egg.

Most kingfisher sightings come in the form of a turquoise streak skimming over the water, but this is not because they are timid birds. Their habit of sitting on branches overhanging water gives many an angler incredibly good views. Kingfishers have been known to sit on the end of a fishing rod held by a silent unmoving human – an excellent perch on which to search for fish in the water beneath.

Dipper

'Water ouzel' and its abbreviated form of 'wizzle' are just two of the local names for a bird that we now call the dipper. This name has been well earned, as dippers constantly bob up and down when perching. They live in fast, shallow and unpolluted streams,

and usually prefer high ground such as the hills of south-west Shropshire. But a few dippers have been seen on the flat plains of the north. First-time dipper watchers should try standing on the quiet bridges that cross the Clun and Teme Rivers. In the spring the birds will be very busy collecting food for their young and may pass under the bridge several times an hour.

Dippers fly very close to the water surface and can be difficult to spot against a dark stream. Their real skills take place beneath the water and are hidden from our view. Dippers feed mainly on aquatic insects and to catch them they walk along the bed of the stream, turning over pebbles and investigating weeds. They travel large distances underwater and a dipper may bob up several metres away from the point where it first disappeared into the stream. Young dippers can dive and swim before they are able to fly.

Dippers build their nests in crevices amongst rocks or tree roots and beneath bridges. The nest is a huge dome made of moss and grass. It usually overhangs the stream, with the entrance facing the water which helps hide the chicks from potential predators. Most Shropshire dippers breed twice in a season, producing an average of five young each time. When spring comes early, they may even have three broods of chicks.

Redshank

Waders are one of the most difficult of groups for identification as they are all 'leggy' birds that share an uncomfortably similar appearance. Even experts sometimes have trouble separating the species. The redshank is one of the easier waders to spot, because its bright red legs are unmistakable. Not that the average walker in Shropshire is likely to come across many, as they are rare here and, like all waders, avoid humans wherever possible.

Redshanks occasionally breed alongside the River Severn and some of its tributaries. The nest is built in grass close to the water's edge and is incredibly well hidden. It is lined with dried vegetation and the long plants around are pulled in and partially woven together to form a concealed cave.
The only real clue to the presence of breeding redshanks is the frantic noise they make when a potential enemy approaches. Out of the breeding season redshanks feed by using their long beaks to probe for insects in wet meadows and mudflats.

Great Crested Grebe

In 1860 a nationwide count of great crested grebes came up with a grand total of forty two pairs left in the entire country. What was once a common bird had been brought close to extinction by an insatiable demand for its beautiful plumage. The grebe's white chest feathers were popular as a trimming for fashionable and expensive hats and coats. Vast numbers of birds were slaughtered to meet the fashion industry's requirements. In the 19th century few people worried about the loss of wild animals, they were seen simply as a natural resource to be exploited by humans.

But not even the Victorians could ignore the plight of grebes, and soon there was a growing call to end the destruction. The grebes' predicament prompted a group of ladies to form 'The Fur, Fin and Feather Folk' a society pledged to stop the unnecessary killing. In 1904 the name was changed to the Royal Society for the Protection of Birds. The grebes directly helped bring about the creation of this important conservation group.

Today grebes have recovered slightly, Shropshire now has around two hundred breeding pairs and the population is still growing. Great crested grebes are confined to lakes, so their breeding territory is restricted. They are found mainly around Telford, Shrewsbury and Ellesmere, with only a few other pairs dotted around the rest of the county. Grebes are not the timid birds that many people believe. They are quite happy to breed in urban lakes. This particular bird was nesting in the centre of Telford. Great crested grebes build their nest amongst reeds. It is a platform of vegetation, often fixed to a sunken branch. When they go off to feed, instead of leaving the eggs exposed, grebes cover them with some of the loose nest material to hide them from the prying eyes of passing predators.

Grebes are exclusively water birds. They rarely fly and are not at all comfortable on land. Their legs are placed right at the back of their body and are perfect for swimming but almost useless for walking.

Coots

These birds have made their way into everyday conversation through a reputation for being bald. This really is a bit odd because the tops of their heads are covered with a conventional layer of feathers and the only 'bald' patch is a white shield that runs down from eyes to beak. Coots are aggressive, argumentative birds that live in loose colonies on water that is well-stocked with aquatic weeds. They prefer large lakes but will sometimes breed on wide, slow moving rivers such as the Severn. They are also often found on clean, undredged canals.

Although they are grazers of underwater plants, coots are not above a spot of piracy. I once watched a coot plunder the nest of a great crested grebe in Telford. It waited until the female grebe swam off to feed and quietly crept onto the floating platform, removed the covering of dead plants and stole an egg by driving its beak through the shell and swimming off. Over two days the coot stole and ate all four of the grebes' eggs. Their food supply is usually less exotic. Around some of the more popular pools in Telford and Ellesmere, almost half of the coots' summer

and weekend diet is made up of stale offerings brought by tourists.

When coots become too reliant on human food, they often breed very close to the spot where they are fed. This gives them territorial rights and quick access to the supply of bread. But sometimes the birds are too confident and the exposed nests are raided by dogs or unscrupulous visitors.

Cormorant

The word cormorant comes from the old Latin name of *corvus maritimus* the sea raven. Zoologically the two birds are not at all related but the large black-looking cormorant certainly does have a brooding raven-like appearance. Cormorants are normally associated with the coast, which is where people usually see them. But most holiday-makers tend to go to the coast in summer, and few realise what conditions are like in deepest winter.

The west coast of Britain, where the majority of cormorants live, is battered by wind and rain during winter and many birds move inland to avoid the worst of the weather. In most years between December and March there is no need to travel to the coast to watch cormorants, they can be seen from a car along the A5 in Shropshire. Nearly every winter finds cormorants settling on the River Severn. Their favourite spot is between Atcham and

Shrewsbury, where they perch lazily on old trees next to the bank.

Cormorants look decidedly out of place in the Shropshire countryside but it certainly suits their needs. The River Severn rarely freezes over and is rich in fish. There are never many cormorants here and they have little impact on the fish population. But that does not stop fish farmers worrying when the birds appear. Several cormorants have been shot in Shropshire, because they ventured too close to commercial fisheries.

These reptilian-looking birds have a reputation for gluttony that dates back many centuries. Today anyone who eats too much is likely to be called a 'gannet', but not long ago the word 'cormorant' would have been used.
This mythology has stuck and people still believe that cormorants would empty a fish pool given the opportunity. But fish is a rich food and a single bird needs only a little to keep healthy.

Reed Warbler

The old Shropshire name of 'water sparrow' is well suited to these birds, as they nest mainly in thick beds of phragmites reeds that grow in shallow water or boggy areas. Reed beds in spring and summer are literally oozing with insects, which provide food for the adults and their rapidly growing young. The reed warblers' nest is quite a feat of engineering. It is anchored onto – and built around – three or four reed stems about a metre from the water surface. This is a safe spot to breed as mink are the only common predators that are likely to venture out into the water. But a different form of danger comes in the shape of cuckoos which often choose reed warblers as hosts for their own eggs.

Reed warblers are found mostly in the east and centre of the county, as their breeding territory is dictated by the presence of suitable habitat. There are important colonies at the Allscott sugar beet factory near Wellington and at Chelmarsh reservoir near Highley. The future of reed warblers is dependent on reed beds, once they were common, supplying raw materials for the thatch that was found on almost every house. Now that tiles and slates are used, reed beds have become a less valuable resource and are under threat. Two hundred years ago they were managed as commercial projects, but reed beds are now left to their own devices. Many are silting over and disappearing while others have been dredged out completely.

Reed warblers are summer migrants that overwinter in Africa, they arrive in May and disappear in early September. They are loyal to their breeding sites and always return to the same reed beds every year. Bird-ringers have been working on the Allscott colony since the 1960s and one bird has been caught and released for twelve successive years.

Overleaf: Reed warbler with chicks.

Sedge Warblers

Like secretive mice, sedge warblers scurry through thick vegetation looking for the insects that make up their diet. They are quiet unspectacular birds that are seldom noticed by passers-by. Because they usually stay inside undergrowth, feeding sedge warblers are much more likely to climb and walk than they are to fly. Sedge warblers, which share their local name of 'water sparrows' with reed warblers, are spring visitors that over-winter in Africa. Some Shropshire birds travel as far south as the Transvaal. They arrive here at the end of April and leave in mid-September.

The name 'sedge' warbler implies that the bird lives around the characteristic grasses that grow close to wet areas. It is certainly true that these birds frequently nest next to water but in recent years they have taken to moving further afield. The conventional sedge warbler's nest is built in extremely thick undergrowth, close to a river or lake.

But they have now been found in hedgerows and scrubland more than a mile away from the nearest water. The nest itself is very difficult to pinpoint. It is often on the ground or just above. The birds approach and leave the site using devious and effective decoy routes. Instead of flying straight to the nest, they often land on a twig two or three metres away. They then drop into the undergrowth and work their way through unseen, often departing by the same route leaving an observer completely mystified about the nest's exact position.

Shropshire's sedge warblers are found mainly around the River Severn and its tributaries, but nowhere are they common. They are an enterprising species and have been known to breed in unlikely areas such as the Stiperstones, where nests have been discovered at the Bog.

Whooper Swan

In spring and summer whooper swans are found far from Shropshire. Surrounded by clouds of mosquitoes, they rear their young on arctic islands in the lakes of Scandinavia and Russia. But once the cygnets can fly, the flocks start moving south before the bad weather begins.

The winter range of whooper swans is difficult to predict. Many fly to Britain and live on the sea, close to the coast where the water is calm. Others take to inland lakes, and a small number may come to Shropshire. Whooper swans are truly wild birds and keep well away from built-up areas. This helps explain why so few people see them; and those that do often get them mixed up with mute swans.

The two species are the same size, but there are other features that help tell them apart. Mute swans have a stubby orange-red beak, while whoopers have a long pointed beak that is bright yellow and black. At a distance the two have very different silhouettes when swimming. Mute swans have an elegant

s-shape to their neck, whoopers hold their heads much higher, giving them a strange stiff-necked appearance.

As a rule, whooper swans are only seen in Shropshire during bad winters. In good weather they keep further north. The name 'whooper' comes from the swans' strange loud 'whoop' call. Whoever coined the old name of 'wild swan' certainly knew their birds, for they are only seen on remote, rarely visited waters; and even there they discreetly vanish before a human interloper gets too close.

Mute Swan

The name mute swan, and its old Shropshire title 'tame swan', have little to do with the real bird. In the wild, away from the tranquil waters of captivity, swans are far from mute and they most definitely are not tame. They have a limited but frequently used vocabulary; they growl, rumble and trumpet during courtship and have a loud alarming

hiss which is aimed at anyone or anything that the swan finds annoying.

There is a popular belief that all wild swans belong to the Queen, but this is just not true. The myth dates back to a time when swans were a highly prized delicacy; swan hunting was a profitable trade and several monarchs passed laws to ensure their supply of swan meat was not threatened. Henry VII imposed a prison sentence of a year and a day on anyone who stole even a single swan egg. Today the Crown technically owns only those swans that live on a small stretch of the River Thames, wild Shropshire swans belong to no-one.

Another swan legend concerns the ferocity of their attack. Since childhood I have heard how a swan can break a human leg with just a single blow of its wings. swans vigorously defend their nests and will use their wings to hit an intruder who gets too close.

Opposite: Mute swan

Having been on the receiving end of such an assault, I can honestly report that it was a painful experience but nothing was broken. There appear to be no records of a swan ever seriously hurting a human.

A swan's preferred habitat is a large lake; they avoid fast-flowing water and small streams, and only live on bigger rivers such as the Severn and Tern. If swans come into regular contact with humans from a very young age they can become remarkably tame and this confidence allows them to exploit a whole new range of habitats. For many years a pair have been nesting on the pool at Walford Agricultural College near Baschurch. The nest is quite close to the B5067 road to Shrewsbury, and every spring traffic is held up as the adults, and sometimes the chicks, cross the road to reach a feeding ground.

Pied Flycatcher

Although these birds nest and feed in woodlands, they are almost always found close to rivers and streams. Once a rare species in Shropshire, pied flycatcher numbers have increased enormously in recent years. Like many small hole-nesting birds, pied flycatchers lack the physical equipment to drill into trees and instead they rely on finding natural cavities or occupy the abandoned nests of woodpeckers or other

big birds. These are few and far between and the lack of suitable sites can restrict the flycatchers' breeding success.

Since the mid 1970s there have been several long term projects in Shropshire which aim to provide artificial sites for pied flycatchers; literally thousands of nest boxes have been erected in the forests around Clun and Ludlow. This has proved to be one of the most successful schemes of its sort anywhere in the country as the number of flycatchers in Shropshire has more than tripled. From the position of having just a few pairs in the 19th century, Shropshire is now one of the most important English counties for this species. Anyone seeing a pied flycatcher in or around their garden should spend an hour making and fixing a sturdy nest-box. There is no guarantee that pied flycatchers will use it but, if they do not, something else probably will.

Pied flycatchers are insect-eating summer visitors that spend each winter in Africa. The bird's 'pied' name refers mainly to the male who has a striking black-and-white plumage, the female's discreet brown and white colouration makes her much more difficult to see in the dappled light of a mature forest.

Reed Bunting

'Reed sparrow' is the local name for this seldom seen bird that haunts reed beds and thick vegetation close to water. They often nest in very boggy areas, where insect numbers are high and mammal predators are rare. This last point is important, as reed buntings build their nests low down amongst grassy tussocks. Away from their usual swampy habitat, nests would be raided by animals such as stoats and weasels.

During the breeding season male reed buntings have a smart black hood that covers the whole of their head, but this disappears in early

of breaking a chicken wishbone and whispering your fondest desire to the largest piece comes from the mediaeval habit of consulting the wishbone of a newly killed mallard. Mystics with a special gift were reputed to be able to read the future of both man and the weather from this simple piece of bone.

The mallard is Shropshire's most widespread and common waterfowl, they are found in all but the smallest lakes but shun high altitudes where the weather is too unpredictable. Although there is only one species, mallard appear to exist in two completely different forms. No urban pool or landscaped lake is without its collection of mallards. These birds are so tame that they miraculously appear whenever visitors unwrap anything that may possibly contain stale bread. This helps keep the birds alive during the worst weather, but perpetuates their reliance on artificial food supplies. Yet on the quieter reaches of the River Severn or secluded private lakes, wild mallard are impossible to approach. In their native state they are extremely shy animals that avoid all contact with people.

They have good reason to be careful, for mallard are a prime target for wildfowlers in the open season. They are prized because they are so difficult to kill and test a hunter's skill to its limit. In some parts of Shropshire, mallard are bred in captivity and released, in the same way as pheasants, to ensure that the population will be high enough for a good shoot.

summer. For the rest of the year males are very similar to females which both become a dull flecked brown and could easily be mistaken for sparrows at a distance.

Reed buntings are resident birds that are with us all year round, although in harsh winters they often desert their usual habitats and move onto farmland and even occasionally into gardens. During the summer they can be found in areas as diverse as the low-lying north Shropshire plain up to the wet patches of the Clee Hills. The River Severn itself is the best place to observe reed buntings, particularly on the central stretches, away from human habitation. This bird was photographed at Chelmarsh near Bridgnorth.

Mallard

The ubiquitous mallard was so familiar to Shropshire countrymen that they gave it the dismissive title of 'wild duck'. The drake alone was called 'mallard', which is an old English term for a male animal. The mallard was always regarded as the most wild of birds, and was believed to be in touch with the elements and the fates. The modern custom

In common with many duck species, mallard females have a subtle and discreetly brown camouflaged plumage, which helps hide them while sitting on a nest. Males, on the other hand, have evolved a bright coloured appearance that is used to attract mates during courtship.

Newts

All three species of British newt, palmate, great crested and smooth are found in Shropshire. The last two species are both known as 'askels'. For some strange reason old county folklore insists that newts have a poisonous bite, which I hasten to say is not true. Although these amphibians need water for breeding, once mating and egg laying is finished they leave the lakes and ponds for long periods, and return only occasionally throughout the summer.

Non-naturalists expect to find newts in water and nowhere else; therefore anything found on dry land cannot be a newt and often these amphibians are mistaken for lizards. Luckily there are differences between the two that help identification. Lizards are smooth and glossy, with very obvious scales, while newts have a knobbly, dull, scale-free skin. The behaviour of the two animals could not be further apart. Lizards love warmth and can be found basking in the sunshine. Newts on the other hand, being amphibians, need to keep their skins moist and avoid direct sunlight. They pass all but the wettest days hiding beneath logs or stones and only come out in the cool night air.

They are often found in damp man-made places such as cellars, eating slugs and spiders. Although newts spend a lot of their lives on land, they are not well suited to the environment, they cannot run or climb easily, they are more comfortable in water where they use their powerful tails as both a propeller and rudder.

Differentiating between the three newt species is difficult as the skin colours that separate them are only visible during the breeding season. Great crested is the largest species and has a much rougher skin than the others, hence its other name of 'warty newt'. The male smooth newt *(bottom, left)* has a wonderful wavy crest that runs down its backbone in the courtship season, but vanishes soon afterwards.

Like frogs, newts have declined because so much of their breeding habitat has disappeared. Great crested newts have now become so rare that they have special legal protection and anyone disturbing them is liable to a very hefty fine. One housing development on the outskirts of Telford had to be stopped temporarily when a breeding colony was discovered. The newts were collected, under licence, and moved to a safe site before building could continue.

Newts are found in obvious areas such as the meres and fens of north Shropshire but, like so many other small aquatic species, they are becoming increasingly reliant on domestic ponds for their survival.

Frog

Not long ago frogs were so numerous in Shropshire that they were a familiar part of the scenery. But that was in the days when every village had its own pond where horses and cattle drank and, in early spring, frogs congregated to breed.

Opposite, top: Frog, bottom: Toad.

Frogs do not live in water, they simply need it for breeding. Once spawn has been laid, frogs abandon ponds and take to dense vegetation where their skin needs to be kept damp, but not wet. Most of Shropshire's village ponds have now disappeared, sometimes robbing the area of its only stretch of still water for miles around. The county is well off for rivers and streams, but frogs do not like flowing water because the spawn and tadpoles are likely to be carried away.

When the ponds disappeared, frog numbers started to drop. Today there is one major hope for the dwindling population and that is the humble garden pool. Water features have always been popular in gardens and now they could not be easier to make. Thick rubber sheeting and pre-formed plastic liners allow gardeners to create a pond in less than a day. Pools are aesthetically pleasing but, ecologically more important, they provide an excellent breeding site for an increasingly rare animal.

Resident frogs pose no threat to the garden, they offer only benefits. Frogs are voracious hunters of slugs and each will eat up to thirty a night, making them useful allies to a gardener striving to protect his prize vegetables. This photograph of a leaping frog shows how the eyes have been pulled back into their sockets to reduce drag, making the leap easier and longer.

Toads

Many people have difficulty telling frogs and toads apart; there is one simple method – frogs hop and toads walk. Frogs are also wet and smooth, while toads are dry and 'warty'. Just like frogs, toads require water during the breeding season but for the rest of the year they do not need to keep their skin moist as frogs do. This gives toads a far greater choice of habitats. They may be included in the 'water' chapter but toads can be found almost anywhere.

Toads often live in dry built-up areas, feeding on garden slugs. They are nocturnal and spend their days hiding beneath logs or stones only to emerge after the sun has disappeared. Their presence frequently goes completely unnoticed by the householder. In early spring toads make their way to breeding grounds where huge numbers can build up. Sometimes there can be literally more toads than water in a popular pond. Even the uninitiated should be able to spot the tell-tale signs of breeding toads. Frog spawn is laid in large clumps that look like tapioca, but toad spawn is laid in long thin strings that often wind around underwater plants.

In Shropshire folk mythology the toad is an unpopular animal, some places still cling to the story that a human can 'catch' warts if he handles a toad. This is a fairy story, the humble toad's only real form of defence is to exude a thick milky substance from its skin when threatened. This substance, harmless to the touch, apparently tastes absolutely dreadful, making the toad an unpalatable meal.

Farmland, Hedgerows & Fields

Farmland, Hedgerows & Fields

Most people's idea of the real English countryside consists of thick hedges enclosing fields full of lazily grazing cattle, while in the distance ripe heads of wheat and barley sway in the breeze. But this is no more natural than a park in the centre of a town, or even a suburban garden. Every scrap of agricultural land has been claimed from forest or moorland and the landscape continually developed and cultivated for generations until, today, it bears little resemblance to the original wild habitat.

Even the farmland around us follows a relatively new design. For centuries agriculture operated on a strip farming system, there were no fields as we recognise them. Different crops, belonging to different farmers, were grown next to each other separated by a narrow band of bare earth, while domestic animals grazed on common land that was open to all. This non-segregated regime made the countryside of the Middle Ages appear very different to that of the 20th century. But during the 18th and 19th centuries Parliament passed a series of complex laws, known as the Enclosures Acts which obliged landowners to mark their land boundaries clearly. Most chose the cheap and efficient method of hedge planting.

The four thousand separate Enclosures Acts ended the open-field system of farming and shaped the field-and-hedgerow landscape that is so familiar today. The nature of the countryside was totally changed.

Today farms are a work place run on sound commercial principles in exactly the same way as any urban factory, only most look a lot more attractive. Farmland has one wonderful side-effect that no other commercial site can match, it provides essential habitats for many of our native animals. Hedgerows are a perfect example. Although they were planted for purely practical reasons, in wildlife terms it is impossible to over-estimate their importance. Ecologically hedges are simply long thin strips of woodland, that act not only as breeding and feeding sites but also as wildlife corridors connecting larger areas of forest, along which animals can travel in safety.

Anyone who visits mainland Europe in search of wildlife is generally struck by the lack of song birds, for the simple reason that hedgerows are seldom found outside Britain. So there are fewer nesting sites for the yellowhammers, linnets and other birds that rely on hedges here. But hedges are only a tiny part of a farm, surrounding them are many other habitats in one small area, and it is this mixture that is so important for wildlife. Birds and mammals can breed and shelter in hedgerows and then search for food in the fields they border.

Shropshire is one of the very best counties for farm-based wildlife. We retain many of our hedgerows, whereas other counties have ripped them out to create ever-larger fields. Many farms are unspecialised and grow a variety of crops that are harvested at different times so the food supply does not all vanish in one fell swoop. The county also has a high percentage of grazing land which, to wildlife, is more 'user-friendly' than intensively farmed arable land. Crops have to be sprayed to keep down diseases and insect pests, they are harvested regularly by huge machines that sweep the landscape, removing the shelter and food supply in a matter of days. Grass fields are less traumatic and more permanent, also, when sheep and cattle are around, the fields are ripe with succulent insects.

Woodland may be a wonderfully rich and diverse habitat but, like every environment, it does have one inevitable drawback: A forest can only support animals that need trees. It is useless to those species that require open spaces. A good mixed farm can offer the best of all worlds. It may contain mature trees for woodpeckers and squirrels, hedgerows for voles and song birds, and fields for curlews and lapwings. Shropshire has a healthy number of these traditional mixed farms, ensuring that their fields support a lot more than farm animals.

Harvest Mice

We have no reliable records about the history of these tiny mammals in Shropshire. They were not even recognised as a separate species until the 18th century, before which they were just lumped together with other small furry creatures and called field mice. But harvest mice are unique in many ways. They are the only animal in Britain with a truly prehensile tail, which can be used as a fifth limb for climbing. They are Europe's smallest rodent weighing just 6gm ($1/5$oz) when fully grown, which makes them vulnerable to a truly huge variety of predators. In addition to the obvious ones such as owls and foxes, harvest mice are eaten by some unlikely creatures like pheasants and blackbirds. Toads have also been seen to swallow harvest mice whole.

The animals' name implies that they live in crop fields, this was true two hundred years ago but things have changed since then.

Opposite: Harvest mice.

With the introduction of huge harvesting machinery, fields of wheat and barley have become decidedly unsafe for tiny animals. Harvest mice are now more likely to be found in the relative security of a thick hedgerow or undisturbed grassy bank. Here they can search for the seeds, nuts and fruit that make up the bulk of their diet. In the spring harvest mice eagerly catch and eat insects such as caterpillars and grubs.

We still do not know the exact status of Shropshire's harvest mice. They are probably rare but the difficulties of finding them are enormous, we are not sure if the dearth of sightings is caused by a lack of animals or our inability to find them.

Voles

Voles are usually mistaken for 'mice' by most observers which is a bit unfair to them as, although they are related, voles are very different animals. Even a quick glance should be enough to distinguish the two. Compared with a typical mouse, voles have small eyes and ears, a very blunt nose, a short tail and hairier coat.

Shropshire has two species of vole that live on land, the bank vole and field vole. Untangling these two is a much harder task.

Bank vole.

Field vole.

Bank voles tend to be a chestnut brown while field voles are much greyer, but individual animals vary enough to make identification tricky based on colour alone. Their names are a help in solving the problem. Field voles prefer to live in areas of open grassland, such as rough pasture. They build a complex series of interconnected runways at ground level, these are often completely covered by grass and provide perfect cover for the voles as they wander in search of food. Field voles breed above ground; in domed nests made of shredded vegetation, they are incredibly well hidden at the bases of grass tussocks.

Bank voles live in hedgerows, woodlands and other areas of dense undergrowth. They do build ground level tunnels if the grass is thick enough but, unlike field voles, bank voles will dig tunnels into the earth, where they can hide and breed. The habitat used by each species produces its own distinct supply of food. Field voles eat grass and seeds, while the bank voles have a far more interesting diet made up of leaves, grass, fruit, berries, nuts, fungi, moss and flowers.

Voles may not be a charismatic or significant species to the human eye, but they are an absolutely essential link in the food chain. They convert plant energy into a form that can be eaten by carnivores; most of

Shropshire's predators rely on voles to some extent. They provide a large percentage of food for species such as kestrels, owls and weasels. A conservative estimate puts the total Shropshire population of the two vole species at around one and a half million. If the voles ever disappeared many predators would die of starvation.

Common Shrew

Known locally as the shrew-mouse, for such a common species this mammal is rarely seen. Shrew sightings are usually so brief that observers often assume they have seen mice. But shrews are not a member of the rodent family and, close to, they look very different. Unlike mice, shrews have tiny eyes and ears, but their most obvious feature is the strange long nose, which is always waving around scenting the air for food and predators.

Shrews are found almost everywhere in Shropshire, living in thick vegetation and feeding on insects. An awesomely aggressive species, they will not tolerate rivals inside their territory; intruders will be met with ferocious attacks that sometimes end in death. Shrews are busy creatures with a very high metabolic rate; each animal eats the equivalent of three quarters of its own body weight every day. A typical shrew weighs around 8gm, so it needs to eat 6gm in each 24 hour period to avoid starvation.

The shrews' need for food has resulted in a strange daily routine; they are neither nocturnal nor diurnal, but have about ten periods of activity every day, each lasting around ninety minutes. Between bouts of food gathering the shrew takes a sleep of about forty minutes, before starting again. Shrews are insectivores that eat worms and other invertebrates. They rarely come into houses because there is little to eat inside. Owls and domestic cats are the biggest threat to the species; but while owls eat the shrews they catch, cats kill but rarely eat them.

Brown Rat

It is amazing how many wildlife books completely overlook rats. They may not be the most attractive or welcome creatures but, in terms of sheer numbers and the effect they have on the environment, rats are one of the most important of all British animals. The brown rat represents the second wave of an invasion that started about eight hundred years ago. Around the 12th century black rats arrived in Britain as stowaways on boats from Europe. Their colonisation of the country had incalculable repercussions, for in their fur they harboured the fleas that carried the Black Death.

For six hundred years black rats were unchallenged; then in the early 18th century their larger and more aggressive relative, the brown rat, arrived by the same route. Within fifty years they had swept across the whole of the country, almost totally wiping out the black rat.

In economic and public health terms, the brown rat is one of our biggest problems in the late 20th century. Many of their predators have been wiped out and, like mice, they are quick to develop immunity to each of the poisons we introduce to control their numbers. Some zoologists speculate that the problem will get much worse unless we discover

a totally foolproof way of reducing the population. Rats live almost everywhere in Shropshire and their numbers are still growing. Each female produces up to forty young a year, and each of these can breed at just twelve weeks old.

As rats spend much of their time beneath ground, in sewers, or abandoned buildings, they often remain unseen. But their effects can be dramatic and wide-ranging.

Weasel

The weasel is one of the most common of Shropshire's predators, but few people ever see one at close quarters. Weasels and stoats are often confused but they should not be. Weasels are truly tiny, no longer than an average pencil; they have short tails with no black tuft to it. Stoats are almost twice the size, with a long black-tipped tail.

Weasels live in a wide range of habitats, but are partial to farmland, where crops are found and mice are abundant. One detailed study showed that a breeding pair of weasels catch around two thousand mice in a single year. As mice raid cereal crops, a family of weasels are helpful allies of the farmer. However weasels are not confined exclusively to mouse-eating, but also hunt voles, rabbits and small birds.

There is little point in setting out to find a wild weasel, even in Shropshire where the population is very high, as sightings are accidental and unpredictable. Sometimes a weasel darts across a road and disappears in seconds, at other times they appear to ignore completely the presence of a human. I once watched a female with young in a wood near Clun. The animals were less than four short strides away from me. The three babies rolled around and bit each other, while their mother sunbathed. They played for several minutes before a dog arrived and the weasels vanished into the undergrowth.

Polecat

Known as the 'foul-marten' because of its strong unpleasant smell, the polecat is becoming an increasingly common mammal in Shropshire. Until the 19th century polecats were widely distributed throughout the country but they suffered terribly at the hands of over-enthusiastic gamekeepers trying to protect gamebirds. Huge numbers were destroyed and the only remaining population was confined to Wales.

Fortunately attitudes have changed and now predators are encouraged more than persecuted. Since the 1950s polecats have slowly spread eastwards from central Wales and Shropshire has become one of their major strongholds. They can produce up to ten young a year and, having no enemies, with the exception of dogs and humans, they have an excellent chance of extending their range even further.

Polecats are nocturnal animals with a well-developed fear of Man. They are more often seen lying dead on the road than they are alive. Increasingly large numbers are killed by traffic but, no matter how big the population, the percentage of animals knocked down remains about the same.

Polecat sightings are becoming increasingly common around farmyards.

So the growing number of road casualties merely reflects the fact that there are more polecats in Shropshire.

Polecats are powerful carnivores capable of taking prey up to the size of a hare, but they will eat earthworms and other small animals when really hungry. The polecat is the wild equivalent of the domestic ferret; the two will freely interbreed given the chance. Many of the Shropshire polecats are the hybrid products of such a mating.

Rabbit

There can be few animals that symbolise the English countryside more effectively than rabbits. A group hopping lazily across a meadow in late evening is one of the most familiar sights to anyone walking the Shropshire lanes. Yet these animals are interlopers, alien creatures that came to Britain less than a thousand years ago. Rabbits probably arrived in the 11th century, brought by the Norman conquerors, not as pets but food. Rabbits were a highly prized delicacy, kept in tightly guarded breeding grounds and cared for by Warreners.

Inevitably some escaped and, being rabbits, soon started to breed. Britain then was a wild and dangerous place; the rabbits faced wolves, eagles and other predators which have since disappeared. The rabbits spread painfully slowly, taking about two hundred and fifty years to reach Shropshire. For centuries their numbers were low, but as their biggest enemies were wiped out, they began to prosper. Soon rabbits were found everywhere apart from forest interiors, wetland and towns.

By the 20th century rabbits had become the most commercially significant wild animal in the country. They were an important source of meat but made their biggest impact through the amount of food they ate. Rabbits eagerly feed on agricultural crops and at the peak of their population it was estimated that they destroyed £2.5 million worth of crops a year in Shropshire alone. Then in 1953 myxomatosis was intentionally introduced. Originally from South America this virus is transmitted by the rabbit flea. British animals had no natural immunity to the disease and 99% of Shropshire rabbits were dead within eighteen months.

Today the virus has mutated and is no longer as lethal. Although native rabbits have acquired some resistance to the disease, it still erupts occasionally and kills hundreds of rabbits every year.

Rabbits live around a complex set of underground tunnels and chambers known as a warren. These are found on the sides of fields, beneath hedgerows and on the edge of woods. But rabbits are opportunists and live anywhere that provides food and shelter. Roadside verges are now a favoured habitat; the M54 is an excellent example of such an unlikely site. Here food is plentiful and the rabbits have more legal right than humans to wander along the grassy verges.

The rabbit population is now at its highest level since myxomatosis arrived. The war against rabbits in Shropshire has been waged for five hundred years, they have been gassed, poisoned, trapped, chased with dogs and ferrets and still their numbers are growing. We simply cannot beat them. It is time to acknowledge the rabbit as a tough survivor instead of seeing it as the 'fluffy bunny' of children's stories.

Mole

Everyone is familiar with the series of soil heaps left by moles excavating new tunnels but few people get the chance to see the animal itself. With its rich loamy soil much of Shropshire is perfect for an animal that spends its life underground searching for earthworms.

Known locally as the 'oont', a fully grown mole can grow to the size of a guinea pig. They have soft velvet-like fur which grows in no particular direction, unlike the usual growth pattern of other animals where each hair is folded backwards and points towards the tail. This strange design helps the mole in its subterranean wanderings, as it can go backwards just as quickly as it can forwards, without its hair causing problems. Country mythology is adamant that moles are blind but in fact they do have tiny, well-hidden eyes that can detect light and movement but not much else. Their main sense is touch and they are highly sensitive to vibration.

Moles are very territorial and defend their tunnel system against rivals of the same sex. When young animals first leave their underground breeding chambers they are often forced onto the surface to avoid being attacked by neighbouring adults. They attempt to escape under the cover of darkness and these young moles form an important part of the diet of tawny owls during the spring.

Moles live for around three years and can make themselves very unpopular with farmers. They sometimes tunnel beneath standing crops, damaging the root system and causing the plants to wilt. Their holes and tunnels can be a potential hazard to stock, sheep have been known to step into mole holes and break a leg. Shropshire moles are most often found in grazing land and deciduous woodlands.

Fallow Deer

While driving home one night on the small roads that skirt Haughmond hill, I saw eleven pairs of glowing green eyes peering at me from the woodland edge. A small herd of fallow deer were on a nocturnal feeding foray. Fallow deer are surprisingly numerous in Shropshire, they are the descendants of animals that once roamed formal deer parks at Attingham, Loton Park, Croft Castle and other stately homes. Some deer also moved in from the south, coming originally from the Wyre Forest.

Fallow deer are yet another example of an introduced species that has become completely naturalised. Precise details about their arrival in Britain are vague, but they have been here at least two thousand years. They were probably first brought by the Phoenicians or Romans. But the population was regularly topped up by new stock carried over from Europe. At first they were confined to parks but that situation did not last long, as deer are masters of escape.

Like most species of deer, it is only the male that possesses antlers; those of the fallow deer are very distinctive as they look like enlarged human hands with splayed fingers. These are grown and discarded annually. They are dropped in late spring, shortly before fawns are born. Fallow deer come in a wide range of colour, from almost white to almost black. In the summer most deer have a heavy white spotting on their coats, but this often disappears when the thicker winter coat grows through.

Shropshire has a unique strain of fallow deer in the Mortimer forest near Ludlow. This is home to the famous 'hairy' deer, genetically they are the same as other fallow deer but this population has a far shaggier coat than is seen anywhere else.

Cuckoo

The call of the cuckoo is the only bird song that is recognised by absolutely everyone. But perhaps not everyone realises that this familiar cry is made only by the male, the female has a completely different sound. Hers is a soft bubbling song, like water being poured from a full bottle. Cuckoos are summer visitors that appear in Shropshire in mid-April. Males arrive before females and for many country dwellers the first "cuck-koo" call of the year marks the true beginning of spring.

In May the countryside seems to be packed with the sound of cuckoos, each trying to intimidate rivals and attract a mate. These calls are powerful and carry a long distance. Cuckoos are rarer than they appear in Shropshire, the county population may be as low as two hundred birds. Mixed farmland is perfect cuckoo territory as it contains the highest number of song birds, a commodity vital to the cuckoo's survival.

Cuckoos are known to lay their eggs in the nests of twenty different species of bird, blackbirds, wrens, robins and skylarks all make suitable foster parents for baby cuckoos. But each female specialises in just one, she enlists the unwitting help of the species that reared her when she was young. She watches carefully as nests are built, then lays her own egg so that it hatches just before those of the rightful owner. A newly hatched cuckoo has just one aim in life, to throw everything else out of the nest.

A female can lay up to fourteen eggs in a season, each in a different nest. Sometimes two cuckoos lay their eggs in one nest and the first to hatch will be the sole survivor. The other will be pushed out of the nest, together with the host's eggs or chicks. Cuckoos are fleeting visitors to Shropshire. The adults stay for a mere three months, before making their way south. The youngsters wait until August or September before they make the long journey to central Africa.

Above: Dunnock feeding cuckoo.
Opposite: Swallow.

Dunnock

This bird is one of the key foster-parent species used by cuckoos. The relationship was noticed by Chaucer, although in his poetry he used the dunnocks' old English name of 'heysugge'. It is from this ancient word, via some tortuous linguistic gymnastics, that we may get the bird's other modern name of hedge sparrow. This name is misleading as dunnocks can be found in almost any habitat that offers thick vegetation for nesting and a good range of food. Dunnocks eat both insects and seeds, and are often seen hopping unobtrusively beneath bird tables picking up the crumbs knocked down by larger more aggressive species. The dunnock population of Shropshire is at least twenty thousand pairs and they live everywhere from the exposed southern hills to domestic gardens. This nest was exposed by a Hinstock farmer who was clearing nettles at the edge of his field.

Swallows

Cuckoos may be the heralds of spring but, for most people, it is the swallow that represents summer. Swallows usually arrive in Shropshire during April and they leave in September. Before we understood the phenomenon of migration, it was believed that swallows hibernated in the mud at the bottom of pools. This idea was connected to the swallows' need to feed heavily before their arduous flight south.

Swallows eat flying insects, which are often found above water. Hundreds of swallows eagerly hunt together over pools and canals in late summer, and the next day they may all have disappeared. Early observers thought that the birds had slipped beneath the water during the night, to find somewhere safe and quiet to spend the winter; in reality the shortening days had triggered the swallows instinct to search for warmer climes.

The marathon migration takes the birds to the tip of South Africa, a round trip of more than 12,000 miles. The swallow population of Shropshire has noticeably dropped in recent years and most experts agree that, although they thrive during their brief stay here, swallows are not doing so well during migration. There have been a series of long, vicious droughts in several parts of Africa. This has effectively reduced the number of insects available to feeding swallows, and has also dried up many of the drinking pools that the birds must visit while crossing areas such as the Sahara belt. Fewer swallows survive the migration and numbers are still dropping.

Swallows are found through the county, avoiding only high exposed ground and built-up areas. The population stands at around five thousand pairs. They usually breed in old buildings, making a cup-shaped nest of mud mixed with grass or straw. The finished construction is as hard as concrete, and is lined with feathers before the four or five small white eggs are laid. A swallow hatched in a Shropshire barn usually returns to the same area to build its own nest, and continues to come back every year for the rest of its life.

House Martin

When we in Shropshire shiver in the winds and frost of winter, house martins, that shared so many of our homes just a few months earlier, trawl the skies of southern Africa for insects. But from the beginning of May onwards they return in their thousands.

House martins build possibly the most visible of all birds' nests. Once a pair have established a breeding site, they collect small mud pellets, wrapped around short pieces of grass or straw. These are clumped together against a house wall, to form a rockhard cup that often stays for several years. The nest is lined with feathers and vegetation as bedding.

A house martin's nest is so well built that it attracts other birds. Sparrows often wait until the nest is finished and then drive off the rightful, but timid, owners in order to lay their own eggs inside.

As our summers become increasingly dry and warm, house martins find it ever more difficult to gather nesting material. We can help by filling an old dustbin lid (or any other shallow container) with soil and water to make a thick mud. The local martins should soon discover this ready-mix and make hundreds of trips each to collect enough to build a nest. A small pile of chopped straw nearby will make the offering even more attractive.

Shropshire is home to one of the biggest colonies of house martins in Britain. But as it is hidden beneath the old Atcham bridge over the River Severn it goes unnoticed. The exact size of the colony changes every year but, at its peak, contained 325 nesting pairs in the 1960s. Hundreds of martins can be seen wheeling over the river in mid-summer, but six weeks later they will all have gone south in search of better weather.

Spotted Flycatcher

For some strange reason this bird is known as a miller in Shropshire. The name seems to be restricted to just this county and I can find no real explanation of how it came to be used. One possibility is that the speckled appearance of the birds' chest could be seen to resemble that of a flour-coated miller.

Spotted flycatchers are migrants that spend the winter months in central Africa and return here at the end of May. Their nests are built behind loose bark, in a hollow tree or amongst thick ivy. But they do show an inventive approach to the choice of breeding sites and will build their nests in the most unlikely places. This pair picked an empty tin can, in a Hinstock garden, that was once used to hold peanuts on a bird table.

Spotted flycatchers have an unmistakable hunting technique: They choose an observation perch and from it launch a series of darting

passes to catch flies in mid-air. The acrobatic flycatcher then returns to its perch and waits for the next victim. If there is ever any doubt about identifying a spotted flycatcher, the distinctive feeding pattern is an infallible guide.

Little Owl

This is a bird of the 20th century that was not seen in Shropshire until 1899, and did not breed here until twenty years later. The little owl is the size of a blackbird, it originally comes from mainland Europe and did not arrive under its own steam. Wealthy landowners on the Grand Tour of the 19th century were very impressed by the perky little owls that they saw in France and Italy. They thought how well these birds would look on their own estates, and many were bought and shipped over for release. After a few false starts the little owl was successfully introduced into Britain in 1874. Because of their diminutive size, little owls had no direct competition for either food or nest sites and they soon spread throughout the south of England and Wales.

At first little owls were not welcome in Shropshire. Gamekeepers believed that they ate the chicks of game birds such as partridge

Overleaf: Little owls are capable of swallowing surprisingly large prey whole, in this case a wood mouse which is longer than the owlet itself.

and pheasant. But a 1930s survey showed that about half the little owl's diet is made up of insects and the rest consists of small mammals. Today they are found throughout the county, occupying almost every conceivable habitat.

They nest in artificial boxes, hollow trees and even down rabbit burrows. Little owls are often the only species of owl that people ever see, for they have a habit of hunting in broad daylight, and sit on high perches such as roadsigns and fence posts. The narrow lanes of Shropshire are superb places to look for the bold little owl. Their county population is probably over twelve hundred breeding pairs, but their numbers have been slowly dropping since the mid 1980s. This could be a natural slump that all species experience occasionally, or it could mean that the little owl has at last finished its colonisation.

In folklore terms these are important birds, for they are the original 'wise old owl' of popular legend. The myth dates back to the ancient Greeks who believed that little owls were the messengers of Pallas Athene, the goddess of wisdom. The association with the 'wise' goddess supposedly made the little owls clever. Today the mythology has come to encompass all owls. The sad truth is that owls are far from intelligent and little owls are not even the brightest of their family.

Barn Owl

At the beginning of the 20th century, the barn owl was described as "the most plentiful of the Owls in Shropshire". A hundred years later population is down to around 140 pairs, this is probably less than one sixth of the number once found here. Barn owls are so rare nationally that they have been given special legal status to prevent anyone hunting them or disturbing their nests.

The old Shropshire name for the barn owl is the 'woolert'. In the not too distant past they were regarded as harbingers of bad luck and even death. Few people could sleep comfortably while a screeching owl remained within earshot. Unlike the haunting melodic call of a tawny owl, the barn owl's cry is unearthly and sinister. It sounds more like an animal in pain than an owl.

Barn owls are not as strictly nocturnal as the larger tawnies. They will hunt in broad daylight if food is scarce or they have chicks to feed. Voles are the barn owls' main prey, but they will eat any small animal that can be caught in their sharp talons. Originally barn owls nested in hollow trees or caves, but they adapted to farm buildings, which offered even greater shelter from the elements and had the added bonus of housing a good number of mice.

Today few owls raise their chicks in hollow trees as, in an increasingly tidy countryside, old trees are likely to be cut for firewood. Barn owls nest mainly in abandoned buildings and barns that are not over-used by humans. People play a major part in the fate of modern barn owls. We are trying to help by making barn owl nest-boxes to replace their traditional sites. This has been particularly successful in Shropshire and is an excellent way of attracting these increasingly rare birds. On the other hand, humans are directly, but unintentionally, the biggest single killer of barn owls. Like many other predators barn owls hunt on roadside verges but, because they have a relatively weak flight, they are not equipped to withstand the air turbulence created by fast moving traffic. Every year in Shropshire up to sixty barn owls are killed by vehicles as they fly across roads in search of prey.

The number of barn owls may have dropped in Shropshire but we have a healthier population than many other counties. Barn owls like the traditional English 'patchwork-quilt' landscape, made up of small fields, hedgerows, copses and meadows

found together in one small area. The mixture gives a variety of hunting grounds, alongside a choice of roosting and nesting sites.

Unfortunately this sort of habitat is rapidly disappearing and in its place comes monoculture, where a single crop is grown to the exclusion of all else. Shropshire's healthy area of mixed farmland is a useful aid to the conservation of barn owls.

Wood Pigeon

These birds were once known as 'quice' or 'quist', a name which comes from the Latin word *questus* – to lament, and refers to the pigeons' mournful call. Wood pigeons are one of the most numerous and obvious of all Shropshire birds, they are big, noisy and very unpopular with farmers and gardeners. Two hundred years ago wood pigeons were

far less common; confined to deciduous woodlands, their numbers were kept down by a restricted food supply. As agriculture became more sophisticated and successful, food became available all year round in the form of arable crops. Wood pigeons moved from the woodlands out into fields and farmers declared war on them.

No-one doubts that wood pigeons eat a huge amount of crops but they have to be admired for their survival abilities. One reason for their success is that the pigeons' breeding season is far longer than that of other birds; it often extends well into autumn. Until the middle of the 20th century wood pigeon was an important source of meat in Shropshire. Local falconers could make a respectable living, selling newly killed birds at small markets. Today we have lost the taste for pigeon meat and the birds are controlled with shotguns. Pigeon shooting as a means of minimising damage does not enjoy the same social status as grouse hunting. It is seen as more of a chore than a sport.

Pheasant

One local name for the pheasant is the 'comet', the bird with the spectacularly long tail. Like so many familiar animals, the pheasant is not a native but an introduced species. These birds originally lived in Asia and legend tells us they were first brought to Europe by Jason and the Argonauts. Captive pheasants appeared in Shropshire during the Roman occupation. They were imported as a source of meat. There is no evidence to show that any of the Roman birds escaped; the pheasants we see now are probably descendants of birds carried here by Saxon invaders around the 9th and 10th centuries.

Today pheasants are an integral part of the Shropshire landscape. They have thrived because of their popularity as gamebirds. Pheasants provided good hunting for many reasons: They were attractive, reproduced readily, were not too easy to shoot and supplied a good meal after the hunt. Once pheasants were adopted as hunting birds, gamekeepers were employed to ensure enough were reared to offer a decent shoot. All possible predators were destroyed and breeding birds were given plenty of food, particularly during the lean winter months.

Today they are still bred in large numbers in Shropshire. Obviously not all birds are shot, many go unnoticed and are left free to wander and breed. The introduction of the pheasant was a boon to large predators, foxes and polecats quickly took advantage of the new food supply. It is impossible to distinguish between the wild and farmed pheasant population and their overall numbers fluctuate dramatically with the hunting seasons. Truly wild pheasants were originally extremely wary birds that kept well away from humans, in Shropshire we now have pheasants that regularly visit gardens to feed from bird-tables.

Grey Partridge

This is the true, original partridge of the British countryside. But it has now been joined by the red-legged partridge, a species that was first introduced around three hundred years ago. The red-legged partridge was brought over from mainland Europe as a shooting bird. Although the interlopers are larger than the native grey partridges, the two rarely compete. To identify the species, look at the plumage: Red-legged partridges are colourful and

had vanished. Now gamekeeping is more enlightened and predator numbers have increased. Inevitably this means that their prey is less fortunate but at least the eco-system is now a little nearer its natural balance.

White-Fronted Goose

The white-fronted goose is one of the most elusive and interesting of Shropshire's birds. They are winter visitors that breed in the arctic tundra of northern Russia and Greenland. Winters are vicious and begin early in those high latitudes, once the chicks have hatched and become independent, northern geese start to move south immediately to keep ahead of the plumetting temperatures.

White-fronted geese are gregarious birds that migrate in groups, they fly in the v-shape formation that is characteristic of the goose family. This helps the birds keep in contact with the rest of the flock and conserves energy for those birds at the back. The geese in front do most of the hard work and their efforts reduce the drag for the birds immediately behind. The leading geese also create a 'wake' similar to that made by a passing boat, helping pull along the following birds. Flight is easy for the geese at the back but tiring for the leading birds, and they often drop back to be replaced by others who have been cruising in the flock behind.

flamboyant with an unmistakable black collar, while grey partridges have a subtle colouration with an orange face that is the same colour as a robin's chest.

The name partridge comes from the ancient Greek expression for 'explosive noise', which is a fair description of the birds' alarm call when a human, or any other predator, catches them unaware. Partridges would rather walk than fly, and when threatened they crouch low and rely on absolute stillness and cryptic camouflage to avoid detection. Only when the enemy is too close for comfort does their nerve break and they take to the air. Few experiences can more effectively shatter the peace of a gentle walk than an unsuspected partridge rocketing out from under your feet, while giving out a stream of loud harsh and rasping calls.

For the rest of the time partridges are retiring, quiet birds when not threatened. They live in any open habitat, such as farmland and scrubland. In Shropshire they are found everywhere but built-up areas, wet ground and thick woodland. Their population, at around two thousand breeding pairs, is about the same as the red-legged partridge and they often share the same range. In the middle of the 19th century the population of partridges was much higher, because so many predators

White-fronted geese come to Shropshire most winters, spending their time on grassed fields. They are grazing animals and the huge areas of pasture lands throughout the county make perfect feeding grounds. This open landscape also allows them to keep a sharp eye open for potential predators. Like all truly wild geese, the white-fronted are extremely wary of humans and are very difficult to approach.

Lapwing

The unmistakable call of the lapwing has given the bird its common name of 'peewit'. Because of their echoing call and highly visible flight displays lapwings seem much more numerous than they are in reality, but unfortunately their numbers are slowly dropping in Shropshire. This is a trend that has been duplicated throughout the country for several years, possibly because of changes in landscape management.

Lapwings lay four eggs in scrapes on the ground, in pasture and arable land this makes them vulnerable to large farm machinery that has little chance of avoiding the well camouflaged nests. Standing grass was traditionally gathered in early autumn, ready for silage but today fields are cut earlier and this either kills the chicks or destroys their hiding places. Young lapwings can run almost immediately after hatching, a useful safety mechanism for a species that nests on the ground. When a predator threatens, chicks scatter in all directions in order to hide, which increases the chance of at least some surviving. This technique is of no help against a harvester.

Shropshire's lapwings reached a population peak in the 19th century when harvesting was carried out by hand. But at that time the birds faced a different threat: Then they were known as 'green plovers' and were the provider of a gourmet delicacy – plovers eggs. Lapwing egg collection was a lucrative business and must have had a significant effect on the birds' breeding success.

Long-Tailed Tit

The long-tailed tit is well named, as its tail makes up more than half its entire length. The bird also has a surprising number of local names. The 'hedge-mumruffin' is one of the stranger titles, more obvious is the 'can-bottle' or 'bottle tit' which refers to the old fashioned bottle shape of the bird's nest. Long-tailed tits make a wonderfully intricate, dome shaped nest, with a small entrance hole in the side. The nest is built of moss and lichen, bound together with spiders' webs and hair. The inside is lined with soft feathers – more than two thousand were discovered in one nest alone.

The nest is built by both male and female, and takes around three weeks to complete. It is hidden in thick undergrowth, deep inside a hedge or shrub. The long-tailed tits' hard work is not confined to nest-building, they can produce up to sixteen chicks in a single brood.

These tits are insect eaters that feed in woodland edges and hedgerows. They are found throughout Shropshire, apart from exposed high ground and open areas with no tree cover. During the summer months, the insect population is at its highest and life is easy. But as winter approaches, food becomes more difficult to find and the birds' energy requirements rise to combat the falling temperatures. Being so small, about the size of a house mouse, long-tailed tits lose heat very quickly. At night they roost together in surprising numbers, up to thirty birds will spend cold winter's nights huddled inside an old nest or nest box, each giving and receiving warmth from those around.

In 1994 some interesting behaviour was seen for the first time in Shropshire. During the winter months long-tailed tits often form

Opposite, top: Long-tailed tit.
Opposite, bottom: Mistle thrush.

feeding parties that scour hedgerows for the few remaining insects, but this time they were seen on bird-tables. Until then long-tailed tits rarely took food from tables but suddenly they seemed to adopt the habit enthusiastically. Since then, every winter, more long-tailed tits have picked up the behaviour. They are particularly fond of finely grated cheese, but this is early days, and the tits are still experimenting

Mistle Thrush

The mistle thrush gets its name from a supposed liking of mistletoe berries, but in reality these are only a tiny part of the birds' diet. Mistle thrushes are also known as 'storm cocks' because of their curious habit of sitting high in a tree and singing loudly during blustery weather, while other birds find shelter.

Mistle thrushes are much larger than their more familiar cousin the song thrush, and they nest in very different places. The mistle thrush breeding season begins remarkably early. They make their nests in solid tree-forks in early March usually before the leaves reappear. This means that they are highly visible and vulnerable, so every year many chicks are taken by cats and other predators.

The Shropshire population of mistle thrushes is around five thousand pairs, and they are well distributed. They are becoming increasingly common garden visitors in winter but rarely come to bird-tables, as they prefer to feed on the ground. Apples are one of their favourite foods, and it is worthwhile wrapping some in newspaper during the autumn and storing them until February when all the windfalls have disappeared. An offering of apples left out on a lawn may bring down a flock of noisy, quarrelling mistle thrushes. This helps keep them alive and gives a wonderful chance to watch them from the warmth of a house.

Redwing

Redwings are a member of the thrush family that breed in Scandinavia and northern Russia. In Shropshire they seem a wild and exotic bird but on home territory they are very approachable. I have seen them nesting at head height in a tree next to a busy shopping street in Helsinki. Like many northern birds redwings abandon their nesting grounds once the short summer ends. The extent of the southern migration depends on local conditions, but every year tens of thousands cross the North Sea to over-winter in Britain. They often migrate at night in huge numbers that can be heard twittering as they pass overhead, completely hidden under the cover of darkness.

There is no normal time for redwings to arrive in Shropshire, because their movements are controlled by the weather. Sometimes there may only be a handful of birds that stay for just a few weeks in January and February; the following year may see thousands of birds that first appear in October and stay until late March. Huge flocks of redwings are a sure sign of bad weather in the north.

Redwings are gregarious birds that feed together in flocks. They are often joined by fieldfares, larger cousins from the north that also come here for winter. At first redwings stay mainly on farmland, feeding on worms in open fields or the few remaining berries on elder, rowan, hawthorn and other trees. Once these supplies are exhausted they are likely to move into gardens, where they can be persuaded to stay by leaving out apples.

They are rural birds that rarely venture into built-up areas, neither do they like wet areas or woodlands. Hills are avoided because they share the cold and windy conditions that the redwing have flown hundreds of miles to dodge. Although there is no real distribution

Opposite: Redwing.

pattern, Shropshire redwings are found in large numbers on the flat plains north of Telford and all around Shrewsbury and Bridgnorth. Redwings have a lovely, soft call that is a mixture of a gentle whistle and random chattering; they can often be heard in early evening as the birds gather in flocks to roost in high hedges.

Slow Worm

Both the name and appearance of the slow worm are traps for the beginner in wildlife studies. They certainly do look like worms or snakes but these reptiles are in fact lizards without legs. There is one simple way to tell snakes and lizards apart: snakes do not have eyelids and cannot close their eyes, while lizards, including slow worms can – and do – blink. There is some controversy about how the slow worm earned its odd name.

One theory suggests that it comes from the term 'slayer-of-worms' , as it was once believed that they lived exclusively on a diet of worms and slugs. We know now that slow worms take a much wider range of prey, including animals as large as common lizards. Slow worms can grow up to 35cm (14in) long and have a beautiful coppery-brown colour to their polished scales. Females have a distinctive dark line down the centre of their backs which is missing from the male.

Slow worms are found throughout Shropshire. They are particularly partial to hedgerows, railways embankments and low-lying scrubland such as Prees Heath. They thrive at Llanymynech nature reserve and numbers have grown to such an extent that slow worms have now moved into local gardens. A long golden lizard, with a healthy

population should be relatively easy to find, but slow worms make observation difficult by building burrows in soft soil or, when the ground is too hard, by using the tunnels of small mammals such as wood mice, in which to escape or simply rest. Along with the common lizard, slow worms have the ability to shed their tail when threatened by a predator.

Unlike the county's other reptiles, slow worms rarely bask in the open; they get their heat by lying under sun-warmed objects such as flat stones. Another favourite spot is beneath pieces of scrap corrugated iron that always seem to be found on farmland. The metal sheets absorb the sun's rays quickly and their corrugated ridges give easy access to a cool slow worm.

Hills, Heaths
& Moorland

Top: The Stiperstones, centre: Prees Heath, bottom: Wem Moss.

Hills, Heaths & Moorland

Geographers will no doubt point out that these three habitats are distinct and should not be treated at as one environment. They are perfectly right but, although the structure of each habitat is different, they share many of the larger and more visible wildlife species. It is for this reason that they have been put together in one chapter.

Hills

When looking at the countryside around us it is always worth remembering that landscapes are living eco-systems that never stay still. They may seem to be eternal but each constantly develops and evolves with the passage of time, going through slow but massive alterations brought about by climatic changes or shifts in the Earth's tilt.

Few places can illustrate this better than the long and chequered history of the Shropshire Hills. For millions of years the Long Mynd was completely submerged under prehistoric seas. Then a series of earthquakes pushed up a huge chunk of land above the surface of the water and the Long Mynd became an island. 80,000 years ago an ice age appeared that helped shape modern Britain. While the majority of ancient Shropshire lay flattened under colossal glaciers, the summit of the Long Mynd jutted out from the ice, a bleak exposed rock standing alone in a frozen wilderness.

When the ice finally melted about 15,000 years ago, the hills were colonised by trees from the warmer south. The Long Mynd was soon blanketed by a huge oak forest that was peppered with ash and elm trees. Man moved in and noticeable deforestation began in the Bronze age. Because of its prominent position the Long Mynd was used as an important burial site for Bronze Age humans from the surrounding area, and there are probably still undiscovered graves lying beneath the heather.

In a mature woodland minerals and nutrients are not stored in soil, but in the trees themselves. When a tree dies and decomposes the nutrients return to the ground and are later re-absorbed through the root systems of other plants. The loss of the Long Mynd's forest robbed the ground of its goodness. Soon little grew and, with its high rainfall, the whole area became waterlogged because there were no trees to take up the water and transfer it into the atmosphere. The few surviving trees and plants died and rotted, and their remains provided the beginning of the peat that now gives the Mynd so much of its character. Since then the higher ground has been taken over by heather and bilberry, with only the occasional hawthorn or rowan to break the skyline.

It is this typical moorland habitat that attracts so much specialised wildlife. Some birds, such as the ring ouzel, will only nest on high moors with low vegetation. The Long Mynd and some of the other high Shropshire hills have become moorland islands in seas of agriculture and forestry. But the natural regeneration cycle still continues and without human intervention, the hills probably would have reverted, long ago, to a woodland habitat. Although mature healthy trees now circle the base of the hills the tops retain their distinctive character because of the grazing sheep that nibble off any saplings that dare take root. This can clearly be seen on the Long Mynd where trees grow up to the point where cattle grids keep the sheep on high land. If it was not for these voracious animals the hills would quickly lose their character.

Mosses

Although Shropshire's mosses are geographically very different to its hills, the two share many similar animal species. The mosses are peat bogs confined to the north-west of the county, they may account for only a tiny fraction of Shropshire's area but these mosses are of international importance. They formed in natural basins that were subject to regular and prolonged flooding. This encouraged the growth of rich aquatic vegetation and when dead, instead of quickly decomposing, the plant material was gradually transformed into thick peat because of the wet conditions. The layer of dead plants formed an impenetrable barrier to the fresh water and minerals that lay in the earth beneath. Standing water stagnated and after a while the developing moss became isolated from the habitats that surrounded it.

Peat bogs are made up of water-saturated soil that is very acidic and low in both nutrients and oxygen. This combination keeps down the number of bacteria present and, as it is these that break down organic material in the 'rotting' process, dead plants decompose extremely slowly in a peat bog. It is possible to dig deep into a moss and gaze at the relatively intact remains of plants that thrived ten thousand years ago. We can even see tiny ancient, tannin stained insect bodies which, in normal circumstances, would vanish within days of death. These seemingly hostile conditions form a unique environment that is home to an extraordinary variety of highly specialised plant species.

Peat bogs are now one of the most endangered of all European habitats. Due to drainage and relentless peat cutting, good mosses are few and far between. In Wem Moss (owned by the Shropshire Wildlife Trust) and the Fenn's, Whixhall and Bettisfield Mosses (an English Nature Reserve) Shropshire has some of the best examples in England and they support an incredible diversity of wildlife. Visitors to Wem Moss need a permit from the Shropshire Wildlife Trust, and there is a public footpath on the eastern side of Fenn's, Whixall and Bettisfield Mosses.

Heathland

For the purposes of this book, heathland is open grassland that is not directly under intensive agricultural management. Technically there are few areas of true heathland left in Shropshire, Prees Heath and Hodnet Heath are two of the best examples. They are based on light, sandy soil which is not really suitable for forest growth. Heathlands are not completely dominated by grass and other low level plants, often there can be larger plants such as gorse and bracken, and even the occasional tree but the overall effect is still one of an open landscape.

Llynclys Hill and Granville Country Park are two of the most accessible of the heathland-like habitats, both are good sites for viewing wildlife.

Raven

This bird's modern name is one of the few that dates back directly to the language spoken by early Anglo-Saxons. A thousand years ago it was called the 'Hrafn', today we know it as the raven. These huge creatures are strong candidates for the title of the world's most intelligent bird and in ancient times they were of enormous importance to the cultures of northern Europe.

Odin, the powerful god of Norse mythology, was known as the 'raven-god', for he had two ravens that acted as spies. They searched his lands for news and returned to sit on his shoulders and report interesting happenings. Ravens also appear in the Bible, and Celtic, Basque and Indian stories.

The flesh-and-blood birds are just as interesting as their mythological counterparts. Ravens have a wing-span of around 1.1m (41in). Once they would have been found throughout Shropshire but are now confined mainly to the county's high ground in the south-west. In other countries ravens can be seen scavenging in rubbish tips but in Britain they have learned to be wary of humans because of extreme persecution. In the 19th century the Shropshire raven population was reduced to just three birds, but now it has risen to thirty five pairs. Ravens in folk stories always nest on high cliffs but the authors of these tales must have done very little research as there appear to be no cliff nesting ravens anywhere in Shropshire, ours breed in trees.

They build enormous nests of twigs wedged into a forked branch, high up in a conifer tree. Ravens are the first birds of the year to show nesting behaviour, often starting as early as mid-February. The massive ravens are surprisingly difficult to find as they are more often heard than seen; their deep hoarse croak is one of the evocative sounds of the Shropshire Hills. And, as ravens are a long-lived species, walkers may see and hear the same birds for much of their lives.

Curlew

Curlews feed in many different habitats; in fields, marshes and moorlands their long beaks probe mud or grass for insects. They are particularly common in damp areas, such as the mosses, and also fields next to rivers. A visit to the confluence of the Rivers Severn and Vyrnwy is usually rewarded with a curlew sighting, and in early winter there are often huge flocks to be seen. During the breeding season, curlews tend to keep further away from humans. Quiet corners of the Long Mynd and Whixhall Moss make undisturbed nesting sites, where curlews breed successfully every spring. There are no secrets being given away here, for the nests are incredibly difficult to find. The large camouflaged eggs nestle on the ground, and the curlews' cryptic colour makes them almost invisible as they crouch low in the undergrowth when a human walks by. Should anyone be fortunate enough to get a close look at a curlew, the female can be identified by her longer beak.

Stonechat

Anyone walking over the Clee Hills or Stiperstones in late spring should catch a glimpse of at least one active little stonechat. With a population of less than thirty breeding pairs, this species is rare in Shropshire; it is more at home at the coast or on larger open spaces such as Dartmoor. Numbers may be low, but stonechats certainly make their presence felt. During the breeding season males find an exposed perch high above the surrounding undergrowth and trill out their territorial song. The nest itself is well hidden on the ground at the base of a gorse bush. In good years stonechats can produce two or even three broods, each containing an average of five chicks. Unlike their close relatives, the whinchats, stonechats do not migrate but stay here all year round. The high hills become very inhospitable in winter and stonechats usually move

Above: Curlew

down to lower altitudes during the autumn. For the next few months they feed and roost in rough vegetation and become very difficult to see, until spring lures them back to the hills.

Linnet

The old Shropshire name for the linnet is 'gorse-bird', earned because of the bird's preference for nesting in the shelter of thick spiky gorse bushes. For centuries linnets were popular cage birds, prized for their musical song. It is estimated that

one quarter of all local families had their own captive linnet or goldfinch. They were regularly sold in Shrewsbury and Wellington markets in the 19th century; all were caught from the wild, a trade that decimated the native population. However when the craze for caged birds disappeared, linnet numbers quickly recovered.

Linnets are now thriving and are found throughout Shropshire. They nest in thick undergrowth, but still choose gorse bushes wherever possible. They are one of the very few song birds that live and breed in loose colonies. Walkers on the Long Mynd in spring may notice only one or two skulking linnets but in reality there may be up to six pairs nesting very close together.

Linnets are also sociable birds out of the breeding season when they form feeding flocks, coming together with chaffinches, goldfinches and other small birds. Linnets roost together at night, again often in gorse bushes. They are primarily seedeaters but take the occasional caterpillar and fly.

One odd fact about the linnet is that some migrate in winter, while others stay put. The migratory birds do not achieve any great distances, some only making it to the south coast, although some Shropshire linnets have gone as far as Northern Spain.

Peregrine

The peregrine is probably one of the top species on everyone's list when it comes to birdwatching. Unfortunately they are also highly prized by egg-collectors, so I will carefully avoid giving any clues to the exact whereabouts of Shropshire's vulnerable peregrines.

The peregrine is the largest falcon in Britain, and one of the world's most widespread bird species. Incidentally the name falcon, until recently, only applied to the female; males

fast and powerful predators. They are known to take over a thousand different species of prey. The peregrine's speciality is its famous 'stoop', when it folds its wings and drops out of the sky at up to 65mph. The chosen prey is killed instantly by a combination of the high-speed strike and a powerful crush from the huge talons. Peregrines will never be common in Shropshire, but it would be a terrible indictment of our care of the county if they were ever to disappear completely.

were known as 'tiercels'. This comes from an old word meaning a 'third', as the male is one third smaller than his mate.
For centuries peregrines were regarded as the ultimate falconry bird; in fact there was a rigidly enforced law that ensured only Royalty and the higher Nobles flew these prestigious status symbols.

Although both eggs and chicks were taken for falconry, until relatively recently peregrines thrived throughout the country. Over-hunting, the Victorian craze for egg-collecting and new forms of pesticide reduced their population to a fraction of its previous level. Fortunately today public opinion and landscape management philosophy are, on the whole, keen to encourage the reappearance of peregrines. Much has been done to redress the balance. For example the nature of pesticides has been changed: They break down more quickly and are less toxic to wildlife. Peregrines, together with many other rare birds, now enjoy full legal protection against any form of disturbance and anyone found raiding a nest is liable to be prosecuted and heavily fined.

Since the 1960s peregrines have made significant progress in their recolonisation of the county, they have now bred here successfully for several years. Peregrine watching is one of the most exhilarating sights of the countryside. These falcons are

Common Buzzard

Buzzards were once birds of the west, although they are slowly and steadily moving eastwards. Today they are regularly seen over Bridgnorth and Wenlock Edge, areas that have rarely seen buzzards over recent decades. Buzzards were driven out during the old days of over zealous gamekeeping, they were killed in large numbers in Shropshire in an effort to protect game-birds. It is unfortunate that more was not understood about bird behaviour in the 19th century. We have now discovered that buzzards eat mainly voles and rabbits, they eagerly feed on carrion when the chance arises but rarely take pheasants or partridges.

Sadly the prejudice against all hunting birds persists even now and every year buzzards are shot and poisoned. They are very vulnerable to this last form of attack, because of their liking for dead rabbits. Unscrupulous landowners are known to lace corpses liberally with strychnine. This is completely illegal and usually kills many other animals along with the intended victim. To our shame, Shropshire has one of the worst records in the country for this sort of persecution.

Buzzards are not difficult birds to find. With a huge wingspan and penetrating 'mewing' call, they are visible from every direction as they soar the skies looking for food on the land below. The name buzzard comes from the mediaeval French term

'busard'. Before this word crossed the
Channel the birds were known here as 'tysca'.

Shropshire buzzards usually build their nests
at the top of strong tall trees; in more rocky
parts of the country they tend to choose cliff-
faces. The plumage of common buzzards is
extremely variable in colour, ranging from
almost black, through every conceivable shade
of brown to light fawn. During the 1980s
there was one buzzard in the Clun area that
was so pale it appeared to be white.

In the mid 1990s a new member of the
buzzard family appeared in Shropshire,
but its exact location is a closely guarded
secret. It has been confirmed that honey
buzzards are breeding here for the first time
in living memory. They are rare throughout
the country and it would be a great coup
if the honey buzzard became a permanent
member of Shropshire's breeding list.

Wheatear

Wheatear is a strange name for a bird that
has nothing to do with wheat and has no
visible ears or ear-markings. It is possible
that the word refers to the bird's white rear,
a patch of distinctive bright feathers at the
base of its tail.

Wheatears are summer visitors to Shropshire,
returning from Africa during March and
April to breed. Nesting is confined to the
hills in the south-west of the county,
the highest population density is found on
Titterstone Clee and Hoar Edge. Only a few
other sites have ever been recorded and there
are probably no more than two hundred and
fifty pairs in total.

Wheatears build their nests in dry stone walls,
inside natural crevices on rocky outcrops and
even down rabbit holes. Burrows also provide

excellent bolt-holes, safe hiding places where wheatears can shelter when threatened by a large predator. They are insect-eating birds and often choose to breed in habitats where sheep graze. Discarded wool provides a warm and soft material for nest lining and insect numbers are high in sheep country. Grazing sheep also keep the turf short, and the wheatears can easily reach the grubs that live on the soil.

Once breeding is finished the birds disperse, to feed before their long journey south, they can be seen almost anywhere in the county. It is a rare August when we do not see a few wheatears feeding in our Kinnerley garden but by mid-September they will all have disappeared from Shropshire.

Meadow Pipit

The two Shropshire pipits, meadow and tree are fiendishly difficult to tell apart. They share similar habitats and both have their strongholds in the south-west of the county. Although the names lead us to believe that the two species are found in different environments, out of the breeding season they are often found living side by side. The tree pipit has earned its name through its habit of perching in trees, while its cousin is more terrestrial. Their choice of nesting habitat is also different. Both birds nest on the ground, usually under the shelter of a grassy hump or other vegetation. Meadow pipits are more likely to be found in the hills, amongst heather and gorse, while tree pipits prefer more wooded areas.

Pipits are, at a distance, dreary looking birds – a prime example of what American ornithologists call 'L.B.J.'s' or 'Little Brown Jobs'. To be more specific L.B.J.'s are dull British birds that are not worth identifying. However at close quarters meadow pipits are beautifully and delicately marked. In the spring the aerial display of the meadow pipit is a common sight over its major breeding grounds around the Clee Hills and Clun Forest. This song-flight is used to establish territorial rights and attract mates. The meadow pipit starts its performance from ground level and flies high into the air before landing, often at the point where it originally took off. During the entire flight, the bird keeps up a wittering song.

Ring Ouzel

Confusingly the old Shropshire name for the ring ouzel is 'blackbird'. In defence of this it must be said that the ring ouzel is very closely related to blackbirds, and about the same size and colour. The only real difference is the huge crescent shape white patch which sweeps around the male's chest. Just like blackbirds, female ring ouzels are brown and although they do possess a crescent, it is much fainter than that of the males.

Skylark

Sadly the melodic song of the skylark is a sound that is becoming ever more difficult to locate. Just three decades ago skylarks could be heard and seen over almost any patch of rough grassland, but their population has dramatically decreased and now there are less than half the number of birds that lived in Shropshire in the 1960s.

They are no longer common anywhere in the county. The skylarks' disappearance is complicated and still not fully understood, we know that it is partially due to radical changes in farming practice. The increased use of chemicals on the land and the introduction of spring ploughing have simultaneously reduced the birds' food supply and threatened the survival of their nests.

The greatest number of skylarks are found where humans exercise less control over the habitat. Hills and heathlands are still relatively undisturbed, so skylarks are free to breed and perform their wonderful soaring song flights. Humans cannot boast of an honourable association with skylarks:

Unlike other members of their family, such as robins and song thrushes, ring ouzels stay well away from human habitation. They only breed on the wilder parts of high hills and moors and even here they are difficult to spot. The ouzel's call, a resonant "tew-tew" which echoes around the hills, is often the only real clue to their presence. Ring ouzels' nests are built on the ground, beneath thick heather or bilberry. They almost always choose sites on steep slopes close to streams.

The Shropshire population amounts to no more than twelve pairs. In recent years all breeding records come from the Long Mynd, only one other site on the Stiperstones has ever been found.

Ring ouzels are summer visitors that fly south in the autumn. They spend their winters in south-west Europe and north Africa, where they still inhabit hilly country. The only chance of seeing a ring ouzel away from high ground is to catch them as they leave their breeding territory. They are very partial to ripe rowan berries and feed heavily on them in early autumn. Ring ouzels can sometimes be seen stocking up on well-laden trees around Church Stretton, building-up reserves in preparation for their long migration flight.

we used to trap them in huge numbers for food. They were also in demand as cage birds, kept for their beautiful voices. There was a barbaric, and completely erroneous belief that skylarks sang sweeter if their eyes were taken out. Unfortunately this was a common practice.

The skylarks we see in the summer are permanent residents of Shropshire but in winter they are often joined by birds from northern Europe. Together they form large feeding parties that search moorlands and meadows for food. In early spring the birds disperse and take up possession of guarded territories in preparation for breeding. The camouflaged nest of a skylark is one of the most difficult of all to find, it is built on the ground and usually hidden by a tussock of grass or heather. Earl's Hill, Cramer Gutter and Hopesay Hill are some of the best of Shropshire's skylark sites.

Common Lizard

The old Shropshire term for this reptile is the 'harriman'; the modern biological name is the viviparous lizard, which means that it gives birth to live young instead of laying eggs. Common lizards are the only member of their family to breed in this way; the behaviour compensates for the fact that they live in a cool and unpredictable climate where buried eggs would be vulnerable to sudden changes in temperature, even in summer. Because unborn lizards develop inside their mother, they are safe from the vagaries of the British weather.

Newly born lizards are almost black but as they grow, they develop a rich pattern of brown, grey and black. Common lizards are creatures of the summer; like snakes they enjoy basking in warm sunshine. As temperatures drop in autumn, lizards find shelter under logs or rocks and then sleep for up to six months, until the warm sun awakens them the following spring.

Lizards can measure up to 15cm (5.5in) long and are surprisingly common. They can be impossible to find, as they inhabit inaccessible places such as the mainline railway embankment that goes south from Shrewsbury. Large numbers are found on the Long Mynd, Llanymynech cliffs and the stone walls around the Clee Hills, but they are rarely seen despite the large numbers of visitors that walk these areas in the summer. Lizards also live in undisturbed gardens, quietly feeding on spiders and small insects.

Common lizards are low slung, ground dwelling animals that are well hidden amongst thick vegetation. They are astonishingly fast and, when disturbed, can vanish in literally a fraction of a second. If a lizard is unlucky enough to be caught by an enemy, it has an ingenious escape mechanism. When the lizard's tail is grabbed, it snaps off near the base. This triggers the tail muscles into a frenetic writhing action.

Most predators turn their attention to the violently wriggling tail, while the lizard quietly disappears. This is not quite as drastic as it first appears, because lizards regrow a replacement tail once the original has been lost. The new one is not as long or graceful as the first but it works perfectly well and can still be sacrificed when an enemy next strikes. There is no limit to the number of times a lizard tail can be dropped and re-grown.

Grass Snake

The grass snake is another of those animals that could have been included in almost any chapter, they are adaptable and can live in many habitats. This snake has just one requirement and that is water; they have no direct need for it themselves but as their main prey is frogs, they must hunt where amphibians are found. The mosses are ideal places to search for grass snakes, but aspiring watchers must be persistent. The grass snake's eyesight is sharp and will detect the slightest movement; if anything large approaches snakes silently vanish into the undergrowth. Grass snakes have no sense of smell, as we know it; they 'taste' the air with their darting tongues and the information is deciphered by a unique organ in the mouth. In common with other members of the family, the grass snake is technically deaf, although it is highly sensitive to vibrations and can feel the footsteps of large animals around them.

Sadly these reptiles are victims of the general hysteria that surrounds all snakes. The fear is unjustified in this case as grass snakes are completely harmless. When threatened their first line of defence is escape but if picked up they may pass an evil-smelling liquid through their anal gland. This is often enough to discourage all but the most determined predator.

Unfortunately grass snakes are still killed because they are mistaken for adders. To tell the two apart, look at their markings. Adders have an unmistakable zig-zag line running along the length of their back, but grass snakes do not have these markings. Every year in Shropshire an estimated one hundred grass snakes are killed by people who mis-identify these harmless animals. There is one hidden difference between the two species: adders give birth to live young while grass snakes lay eggs.

Adder

The local name for the adder is 'etther' and in Shropshire, as everywhere else, it has a reputation that has absolutely nothing to do with reality. Adders are far more frightened of humans than we are of them: the size difference alone is enough to terrify the poor reptiles. Adder encounters are usually the result of sheer chance; normally an adder feels the vibrations made by the heavy footsteps of an approaching human and disappears before it is seen.

Of course it is true that adders have a poisonous bite, but it is designed to kill the mice and voles that make up the snake's diet. Adders very rarely attack humans, and when they do the bite is seldom fatal. Death normally occurs as the result of a specific allergy to that particular venom or if the victim suffers from another medical problem, such as a heart condition, which is aggravated by the bite. For the majority of people an adder bite is only a little worse than a bee sting, with localised swelling and symptoms reminiscent of 'flu. But if bitten by an adder, it is always necessary to see a doctor as soon as possible.

High moorland, such as the Stiperstones and the Long Mynd, and the lower lying mosses are perfect adder habitats. They exist in other areas but are extremely difficult to find when hiding in a hedgerow or woodland. Early morning is the time to look. Snakes are cold-blooded which means that they do not generate their own body heat, as birds and mammals do. A cold night reduces a snake to a cool lethargic lump. Before hunting it must take in energy from an external source, so they absorb heat by sunbathing. In the early morning, adders find south facing banks and bask in the warmth of the rising sun, becoming increasingly active as their temperature increases.

Overleaf, top: Grass snake, bottom: Adder.

Built-up Areas

Telford Town Centre

Built-up Areas

The phenomenon of urban wildlife is hardly new; some animals have lived alongside man for thousands of years. In the Middle Ages kites scavenged in the streets of British cities. It is happening all over the world; in the USA raccoons raid dustbins and many Australians have been woken by noisy, nocturnal possums climbing in through windows in search of food. Every year sees more species take the first tentative steps towards urban life. Growing numbers of badgers are becoming town-dwellers, when their setts are encompassed by development. Within a single generation they learn to accept the proximity of human habitation.

Many first-time observers often wonder why animals choose to live in built-up areas, when they could stay in the 'wild'. But animals do not view the world in quite the same terms. There is nothing natural about the British landscape. The fields, hedges, canals and other features that make up our countryside are entirely man-made, just like a town centre.

Animals never judge a habitat on its appearance, they must be more practical in order to survive. Food, shelter and breeding sites are the only real consideration and some towns offer these in abundance. Not all animals are suited to urban life. Some species are so wary of humans that they never venture close to built-up areas. Others are specialised in their feeding requirements and could not survive in a town because food would be impossible to find. But many animals have learned to tolerate the presence of Man and now take full advantage of our activities. For these adaptable species towns offer rich pickings. Built-up areas all have their share of abandoned buildings, parks and unused garden sheds, any of which would make excellent shelters for animals. Wildlife in towns is also less likely to get shot, poisoned or chased by dogs than its rural counterpart. And, with the exception of domestic cats, there are fewer large predators in towns.

However the real prize comes as food. Humans are an appallingly wasteful species. In the West, at least, we throw away almost as much food as we consume. We may not recognise our rubbish as food, but the animals around us certainly do. Dustbins, bird-tables, waste tips and even the pavements around fast food shops are all worthwhile feeding grounds for urban wildlife. For some species there is a simple formula that dominates their existence: Humans equal food. As towns grow, so does the population of wild animals that live there.

Foxes often scavenge roadside verges, in search of small animals killed by traffic.

Fox

There really is no single habitat in which to put the fox. They are one of the world's most adaptable and intelligent animals. Not only are foxes found in every recognised habitat in Britain, they have been successfully exported to Africa, Australia, North America and countless other destinations. Foxes are quite simply born survivors. Although they live throughout Shropshire, the best place to see a wild fox is in a larger town. Surrounded by the sight, sound and smell of humans, they are less nervous than their rural cousins.

Unlike farmers, who see the fox as a predator threatening the survival of livestock, townspeople often welcome the fox as a wild link with the countryside. In every large town in Shropshire wild foxes are deliberately fed by

humans. Over time, they come to expect these easy meals and can be taught where and when to collect food from a lawn or patio. Not everyone welcomes urban foxes as they can be a problem, particularly when rubbish is collected in flimsy plastic bags which can be ripped open by a hungry fox. The introduction of wheelie-bins has largely stopped these raids.

Foxes are a useful addition to Shropshire's street life as they help keep down the population of rats and mice. There are some cat-owners who fear that blood-thirsty, ravenous foxes will make off with their pets, but this is extremely unlikely as foxes are nowhere near as big as many people think. Domestic cats are often heavier than foxes and, armed with razor-sharp claws, are far better equipped for fighting. Very few foxes would stand up to a fully grown cat.

Inevitably town foxes have to pay a price for their lifestyle and it comes in the form of road traffic. A recent survey shows that 80% of urban foxes are hit by cars at least once during their life; road traffic is by far their biggest killer. The foxes themselves do not help the statistics. There are two traffic islands in Telford where foxes breed every spring. To reach their earths the foxes must cross two lanes of busy traffic, and they do not always succeed.

Hedgehog

Known locally as the 'urchin', hedgehogs can be found almost everywhere in the county with the exception of wet and high ground. Most people associate hedgehogs with gardens, for the good reason that these provide the best feeding opportunities. During the day they curl up and sleep in hedges, shrubs or compost heaps. At night they come out and feed. Hedgehogs have learned to search around bird tables, picking up scraps beneath.

The wide variety of plants grown in most gardens attract a huge number of slugs, one of the hedgehogs' most important foods. A single hedgehog can eat one hundred slugs in a single night and gardeners should welcome the animals for this service alone. They can be encouraged to stay with extra food, but please do not leave out the traditional bread-and-milk offering as it has

disastrous effects on their digestive system. Cat food makes an excellent meal for hedgehogs, but it is best to wait until the hedgehog appears and give the food directly to the animal itself rather than leave it out as a gift for the local cats.

The thick forest of spines is the hedgehogs' best defence against predators and has worked efficiently for millions of years. But towns are home to one enemy that is impervious to such armour. The biggest killer of hedgehogs is road traffic and recent evidence shows that, in Shropshire, some hedgehogs are learning to adapt to the new threat. Rural hedgehogs obviously face less traffic and they respond to a speeding vehicle exactly as they would to a badger, by curling up. Caught in the path of a giant lorry the hedgehog's fate can be imagined. Urban hedgehogs are becoming street-wise. Faced with a fox, they roll into a tight ball but when threatened by a lorry they run. This is a fascinating example of learned behaviour in response to changed circumstance.

House Mouse

Along with humans and brown rats, this is the most widely distributed mammal on Earth. But whereas rats need a nearby supply of drinking water, house mice can live successfully without it as they get their minimal moisture requirement from the food they eat. As a result house mice can live virtually anywhere, although in the late 20th century they are not terribly fond of houses. In earlier times houses were ideal for mice, they offered shelter against the elements and contained few predators but, best of all, they provided an endless food supply. But that was in the days when food was stored in sacks or boxes, containers that offered no protection against the sharp persistent teeth of hungry mice.

Kitchens are very different now, food is kept in freezers and tin cans which are invulnerable

even to mice. However this minor detail does not altogether deter such inventive creatures, they simply turn their attentions to other, less likely food supplies. Out of choice house mice eat seeds and grain but they have been known to feed, and survive, on such strange items as plaster, soap, leather shoes and hardened glue. It was in the Ironbridge Gorge that one of the first strains of 'super-mouse' was discovered. For decades poison was laid to control the mice but not only did they develop an immunity to it, they actually ate it and thrived. Since then new forms of poisons have been introduced but it will not be long before the mice learn to cope with those too.

Genetic adaptability is the secret of the house mouse's success. It takes most mammal species many generations to alter their body chemistry or anatomy in response to changes in their surroundings, but house mice can do it with astonishing speed. A small population were

trapped in a cold storage unit in Telford; immediately each of the mice responded by growing thicker fur. They successfully bred and their offspring had even thicker fur. Like so many of our most successful species, the house mouse is not native. They originally came from the Middle-East and probably arrived here sometime around the Iron Age, some three thousand years ago. They were the first animal to be introduced into Britain by humans.

Long-Eared Bat

Of all our wild animals, bats are the most misunderstood and maligned. Yet people who are frightened of bats have probably never really seen one at close quarters. This is a great shame, for bats are well worth looking at and are certainly not the repulsive creatures of legend. Bats form the order of 'chiroptera'

which means hand-wing, they are the only mammals living on earth that are capable of true powered flight.

The most numerous and widespread of Shropshire's bats is the brown long-eared. They are completely unmistakable as their huge ears make up almost half their entire length. Like all British bats, this species lives exclusively on insects. They have a very high metabolic rate that demands an enormous amount of food. A single bat may eat up to seventy moths in a night. For this reason alone, bats should be cherished by gardeners for without the help of hungry bats, the number of caterpillars would rise dramatically.

Long-eared bats are often found in domestic attics; stories of bats living in belfries are rarely true. Churches are generally cold, draughty and noisy. Bats are highly intelligent animals that long ago discovered the benefits of living above a centrally heated room. Roosting bats should be treasured because all species, even the long-eared, have suffered over the past few decades. They now have complete legal protection against any form of disturbance, which is why the entrance to Kynaston's cave on Nesscliffe Hill is locked when roosting bats move in during the summer months. Some bats return every year to familiar roost sites, they are a long-lived species and one female achieved the ripe old age of thirteen years.

Bats sleep through winter, when their food supply disappears. Long-eareds usually hibernate in hollow trees or attics. British bats are completely harmless to humans; unlike mice they do not transmit diseases or chew through wires and carpets. Some bat species can be encouraged into gardens through the use of wooden roost boxes, which have openings at the bottom instead of the familiar side holes in a bird box.

House Sparrow

To the average town dweller, house sparrows must seem to be the most numerous of all Shropshire birds. But the sparrows' omnipresence is deceiving; chaffinches and wrens both have far higher populations but they lack the sparrows' special affinity for man-made habitats and are therefore less visible. House sparrows earned their name from a habit of nesting in attics, behaviour that was also responsible for the bird's local name of 'Thack' or 'Thatch sparrow'.

House sparrows are closely related to the weaver birds of Africa. This should be obvious to anyone who finds one of the sparrow's 'wild' nests built deep inside a hedge. These are tightly woven domes of grass and twigs, with a small entrance hole in the side. Most urban sparrows are too street-wise to build outside nests; they use buildings for rearing their young. Sparrows are specialists in making nests under eaves, where a small amount of grass provides a soft bed for the chicks, but it is the solid man-made roof that keeps off the wind and rain.

Town sparrows benefit enormously from their association with humans. Their breeding season is longer as their chicks are well protected from the elements and food comes all year round. Technically house sparrows are seed eaters, but just watch them at a well stocked bird table. Sparrows will devour almost anything that is edible and this is one the secrets of their success.

Swift

'Jack Squealer' is the old Shropshire name for this strange bird. It comes from the swifts' unearthly courtship scream which is as its loudest shortly after they return from a long winter in Africa. Swifts arrive in late April and disappear again within four months; in that time they mate, find a nest site and rear an average of three chicks. Swift is an apt name, in every sense, for they are one of the fastest of all British birds.

Swifts spend most of their lives in the air, they eat, sleep and even mate in flight. Their short, weak legs are not at all suited for walking, although they can cling tenaciously onto a vertical house wall. Should a swift have an accident and be forced to land on the ground, it cannot take off again. These birds need to launch themselves into space from a high take-off point. On the floor their legs are completely hidden, early observers thought that they had none at all. The Latin name for the swift is *'apus'* which means 'without foot'.

Kestrel

Often called the 'windhover' because of its ability to remain stationary in the air while searching for small animals hidden in the undergrowth beneath, the kestrel is the most successful bird of prey in Shropshire. Few drivers travelling on the M54 will not have noticed one of these hovering falcons poised high above the grassy verge, and the lucky ones will even see a kestrel slip sideways to drop soundlessly onto a mouse beneath.

In the late 1950s kestrels were becoming increasingly rare. They had been persecuted by gamekeepers for decades, falsely accused of taking young game birds. Following the war there was a terrible overuse of powerful agricultural pesticides, such as DDT, which entered the food chain and contaminated the small animals on which the falcons fed. Thousands of kestrels died of poisoning in this county alone. When the worst of these pesticides were banned their numbers started to recover.

In rural areas kestrels nest in hollow trees or cliff ledges but in towns they breed in unused chimneys and undisturbed window ledges. One factory in Whitchurch had the privilege of housing a breeding pair inside an air-conditioning unit, where they successfully raised three chicks. Kestrels prefer hunting in open spaces and they have benefited from

They are capable of flying at around 60mph which makes it easy for them to travel long distances in search of food.

Before humans unintentionally provided nesting sites in the form of buildings, swifts were confined to breeding in caves, cliffs or hollow trees. In 20th century Shropshire they appear to have completely abandoned this behaviour in favour of nesting in houses. Old buildings provide the best sites, as they are more likely to have the loose tiles or missing bricks that act as entrance holes into the roof space. New houses are more secure and have fewer entry points. Towns with lots of old buildings, like Shrewsbury and Bridgnorth, supply an almost endless choice of nest sites. But built-up areas are not ideal places to hunt so swifts commute, every evening they can be seen hawking the skies above rocky outcrops on Grinshill and the Stiperstones, catching the small insects carried aloft by hot air rising from the sun-warmed cliffs.

the creation of new roads and urban parks, which both offer good hunting territories. At around eleven hundred breeding pairs the kestrel population in Shropshire is healthier than it has been for a long time.

Song Thrush

The local name for this bird is the 'throstle' and in Shropshire it was once eagerly hunted for food. For many people the song thrush is the classic 'English-garden' bird, without which no lawn is complete. In spring and summer short grass attracts thrushes as it is a perfect place to catch worms. Unfortunately many gardens no longer have resident throstles, because the song thrush population has dramatically dropped over recent years.

There are many reasons for the thrushes' decline. A series of long, hard winters during the second half of the 20th century killed many birds. An increase in the use of garden pesticides is also to blame. Slugs and snails form a major part of the song thrush diet, pesticide pellets either wipe out their food supply or, in the worst cases, poison the birds when they eat contaminated prey. As a result the best places to see song thrushes today are in municipal parks where pellets are not used for the safety of playing children.

The song thrush is unique amongst British birds, for it is the only species that uses an anvil to reach its food. Snails are a prized delicacy, but their hard shells are impenetrable to the thin beak of a song thrush. So, instead of wasting time attempting to winkle them out, the song thrush picks up a snail and thumps it against a convenient stone. This smashes the shell and exposes the soft body inside. Thrushes tend to use the same stone regularly and they can easily be identified as anvils because of the pile of shattered shells that are scattered around.

Opposite: This kestrel was photographed on the A442 near Telford Town Centre.

Black-Headed Gull

The name 'sea-gull' is now definitely obsolete, ornithologists simply refer to the family as gulls and the reason is simple. There are some gulls which have not been anywhere near the sea for many generations and the black-headed gull is the best example. Shropshire has a number of breeding colonies of black-headed gulls but their status is constantly changing.

Perhaps more than any other bird, they are able to change behaviour as local conditions alter. If the food supply dwindles or humans become too common, entire colonies will abandon traditional nest sites and move to a new area.

They breed in colonies, where each pair makes a cup shape nest directly on the ground. This makes them vulnerable to attack from predators such as mink. During mild winters, black-headed gulls stay in Shropshire, but if the weather deteriorates they simply move south. In winter the birds lose their distinctive chocolate brown hood and in its place there is just a dark smudge behind the eyes.

Black-headed gulls are just as likely to be seen foraging on farmland as they are to be floating on a Telford lake. They have also learned to scavenge food from tourists at Ellesmere or on the River Severn. Gulls are bright and agile, and often outwit ducks and geese by catching bread in mid-air, before it hits the water. Black-headed gulls are much smaller than any other gull we might see in Shropshire and their dirty orange legs makes identification simple.

Robin

This really is one bird that needs no introduction. With the exception of the most hostile, wind-swept habitats, robins are found virtually everywhere in the county. Historically robins were birds of deciduous woodlands, but a highly adaptable nature has enabled them to alter their behaviour and make full use of their unique position in the popular culture of an English garden. Householders often become very possessive over 'their' robins and go to great lengths to feed them. For future reference robins are particularly fond of meal worms and grated cheese.

Many people are proud of their tame robins and tell visitors that the same bird has lived in their garden for years. Unfortunately this is rarely true as few robins live longer than eighteen months. However tame behaviour is sometimes passed on from generation to generation. It has been proved that when

Below: Garden pools are useful drinking stops for birds such as this robin.

gardeners think they are feeding a single long-lived robin, they are in fact feeding a succession of six or seven generations.

In many Shropshire gardens, robins have become so tame that they will land on an outstretched human hand, if it contains food. The bold approach of garden birds is very different to that of robins that live in remote woodlands for they are still remarkably timid animals. Spade following is a unique piece of robin behaviour. Humanised robins quickly notice when a gardener comes out to dig over the soil, they know that his activity will expose a huge number of creepy-crawlies. They sit and watch patiently as each shovelful is turned over, pouncing when a worm or insect's larva is unearthed.

The friendly robin of popular folklore bears little resemblance to the real bird. Robins are tough and extremely aggressive to members of their own species. Even out of the breeding season, any robin that trespasses onto the territory of another runs the risk of being attacked.

Collared Dove

The collared dove's story is one of astonishing success. They have colonised Britain in a spectacular way that has never been matched by any other bird. They were originally an Eastern European species that gradually spread its range westwards. They first began to appear in this country in the 1930s but did not breed successfully here until 1955. They started in the east, and Norfolk became their first stronghold, but the westward movement was relentless. Collared doves were not seen in Shropshire until 1961, when they appeared in Atcham. Two years later they started to breed.

Collared doves are now found throughout the county, and have reached a population of around four thousand breeding pairs. They are closely associated with man-made habitats and are most often seen around

Church yards make excellent feeding and nesting sites for collared doves.

gardens, parks and farms. Along with their larger relative the wood pigeon, collared doves are very much at home in towns. Shrewsbury and Telford have thriving populations. Not everyone welcomes these doves as they have an extremely loud monotonous three note call, and they are at their most vocal shortly after dawn. Many town dwellers lose their affection for these pretty birds when they are woken at five o'clock in the morning by a resident pair of doves re-enforcing their territorial rights for up to an hour at a time.

Magpie

Locally this bird was called simply the 'pie', after its distinctive black and white plumage. 'Mag' was added later, and derived from the term 'maggie' which was another name for a chatterbox. No doubt this was a reference

to the magpie's incessant croaking, maintained even when alone. Magpie may be the official title of these birds, but less polite names are often used, for magpies are deeply unpopular birds. They have always been seen as harbingers of bad luck and today they are portrayed as cruel killers.

Magpies are corvids, closely related to crows and rooks, and are extremely intelligent and adaptable. Like all corvids they feed on a remarkably wide variety of foods, ranging from carrion to seeds. In recent years they have been accused of the mass slaughter of song-birds. It is true that magpies will raid nests and eat both chicks and eggs, but this is opportunistic behaviour and only forms a small part of the bird's diet. It is grossly unfair to blame magpies exclusively for the loss of Shropshire's small birds.

Because they are so very intelligent, magpies have discovered a new food supply that is easy to exploit and therefore much more attractive. They have learned to scavenge from humans. Magpies know exactly where to find the best bird-tables and quickly work out when food is put out. They wait until the human disappears, swoop down and, with their huge beaks, collect a mass of food before flying off to eat the booty in solitude. The whole process is over in a few seconds.

Every part of Shropshire has reported an increase in the number of magpies and their population may be as high as ten thousand breeding pairs. They rear their young in massive domed nests built deep in thick undergrowth, particularly hawthorn bushes. The magpie's interest in shiny objects is no myth. Lying inside the nest, and sometimes actually built into the structure itself, can be found bottle tops, silver paper and, in one Bridgnorth nest, a silver necklace. This explains one other local name for the magpie – 'the thief'.

Jackdaw

The jackdaw is the smallest member of the crow family in Shropshire, but they are every bit as clever as their close relatives. Traditionally jackdaws nest in hollow trees and cliff-holes but now there are far better sites, in much higher numbers and in all shapes and sizes. Humans may be under the impression that chimney pots are a convenient way of piping smoke from our fires, but jackdaws know better. Chimney pots are highly desirable residences that are perfect for laying eggs and raising chicks.

Jackdaws start nesting in spring, just at a time when open fires are being abandoned due to the warmer weather. The jackdaws collect sticks, feathers, sheep wool and anything else that might make a warm soft nest. After a winter of fires, chimney pots are bone dry when the assorted lining is added, no bird could ask for more. Unfortunately, once the nesting season finishes, jackdaws do not remove their nest material and it can become a fire hazard. When the cool autumn evenings return, many people light the first fires of the season, unaware of the fact that their chimney is stuffed full of dry sticks. Every year there are dozens of fires caused by rising sparks igniting the jackdaws' nest. If the chimney is not used, nesting jackdaws pose no threat but a working chimney pot should be covered with a wire cap.

Walkers on the Long Mynd can see literally dozens of jackdaws hopping around the sheep-cropped turf. The birds are there to collect the insects that live around sheep and, as a bonus, they also pick up the scraps that visitors discard when their picnics are finished. Long Mynd jackdaws may seem the epitome of rural birds but at dusk, when the weather is cold and windy or during the breeding season, they move downhill and spend the night in the relative warmth of Church Stretton.

Opposite: Jackdaw

Carrion Crow

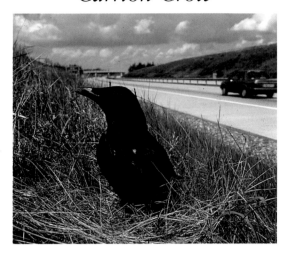

The carrion crow is cursed with a name that is guaranteed to win it few admirers. While it is true that these birds do have a liking for eating corpses at various stages of decomposition, they are also skilled foragers and hunters. Like other corvids, crows are true omnivores that eat almost anything that is vaguely edible which helps explain their enormous success. The Shropshire crow population is around twenty thousand pairs and they can be found everywhere from town centres to the high hills. With a diet that includes carrion, insects, seeds, eggs, birds and small mammals, fruit and worms, it is not surprising that crows should be able to thrive in almost any environment.

Many people have problems telling crows from their close relative the rook. The easiest way is to look at the birds' heads, crows have a solid black beak while rooks have a very obvious white cheek-patch that covers the entire base of their beak. Their nesting behaviour is also different, rooks breed in large, noisy colonies made up of dozens of nests built very close together, that are impossible to miss by even the most inexperienced bird-watcher. Crows, on the other hand, are less sociable and their solitary nests are usually built in the highest possible tree in their territory. These nests can be very difficult to find.

Until recently most farmers and gamekeepers carefully searched woodlands for breeding crows, and a shotgun blast through the bottom of the nest ensured that the population would not grow during that particular year. Attitudes have now calmed and the crow has become a less persecuted species, although it is unlikely that the Shropshire population will grow, as it is probably already at saturation point.

Siskin

Siskins are birds of the winter in Shropshire. They are an interesting addition to the growing list that rely on humans in bad weather. But siskins rarely take food directly from tables, they prefer to join the more acrobatic species and feed from a suspended peanut bag. This requires a delicate hanging and probing technique that matches the

siskins' normal feeding behaviour. In the wild their diet is made up mainly of alder seeds which are tricky to remove and often demand some highly athletic contortions before the bird is rewarded.

Alder seeds are plentiful in the first few months of winter but when they are all eaten, many of the birds turn to gardens, where they stay until the end of winter. Siskins did not eat peanuts until the early 1960s. The first birds took nuts from red plastic bags which was simply a random choice, but even now, given the choice, siskins will usually feed from red bags rather than any other colour.

There is no real chronological pattern to the siskins' feeding behaviour, much depends on the weather and availability of the alder seeds. During some winters siskins are few and far between, while in others there are literally thousands. Most Shropshire siskins breed in Scotland or even Scandinavia.

When the weather is bad they move further south; when it is mild they stay put. By late March most siskins have started to move northwards but a small number remain in Shropshire to breed. Siskins nest in conifer trees, building delicate nests of grass and moss, usually towards the end of high branches. Summer siskins are still a rare sight in Shropshire; they are widely – but very thinly – distributed throughout the county. But as the national population is steadily growing and expanding its range, it is likely that ever more siskins will stay to breed here.

Blue Tit

Inevitably this bold and attractive bird has collected many nicknames in Shropshire: 'Tom Nouf', 'Tom Tit', 'Blue Bonnet' and 'Billy Biter' are the best known. The last of which comes from the bird's pugnacious ability to defend itself; a blue tit will fearlessly peck

at anything that interferes with it, particularly when nesting. If blue tits were less common, bird watchers would probably travel many miles to see them, for they are surely one of the most beautiful of all our birds. They are so familiar that we tend to take them for granted, but blue tits are acknowledged to be amongst the most spectacularly colourful birds in the world.

Blue tits evolved for life amongst mature deciduous trees and they still thrive in Shropshire's woodlands, where they spend up to sixteen hours a day searching for insects in the canopy. But over the past two hundred years they have moved into parks and gardens where their natural curiosity allows them to take full advantage of completely unexplored opportunities. While some species never truly lose their fear of humans, blue tits are confident and inquisitive. They quickly accept the presence of humans and learn to exploit all feeding possibilities. They are pioneers that are the first to investigate new nut-bags or fat-filled coconut shells. Their activity attracts other species who follow the blue tits example.

Because of their acrobatic and entertaining habits blue tits have been voted the most popular garden bird, beating even that perennial old favourite, the robin.

Great Tit

Shropshire's three known colloquial names for the great tit, 'Tom Noup', 'Ox-eye' and 'black-headed tomtit' have all been recorded. 'Ox-eye' is reputed to copy the sound of the great tit's song. The origin of the bird's better known name, great tit, is an interesting tale. Tit is an abbreviation of titmouse which, in itself, is a twisting of two even more ancient words. Mouse comes from 'mase', an old English word for small bird, and tit is from 'tittr' which means small.

Opposite: Great tit.

Great tits are found almost everywhere in Shropshire, with the exception of completely tree-less countryside. They are woodland birds that are quick to seize new opportunities. Inside forests great tits tend to stay high in the trees, well away from humans, but some have moved into gardens to enjoy the good life, especially in winter. As insect-eaters, great tits have a bleak time in cold weather when their food supply all but disappears. Even the most meagerly stocked bird table can literally make the difference between life and death. Great tits are not travellers and once they move into a garden for food, they often establish territories and stay to breed.

New gardens frequently lack suitable nesting places for small birds; great tits have particular difficulties as they prefer holes in mature trees, a feature missing from many small gardens. Traditional sites can be re-created easily with a nest box. Anyone who feeds birds in winter, should finish the job by providing those same birds with a suitable breeding place in the spring. This really does help the local bird population.

Starling

There can be no-one in Shropshire who has not noticed starlings at some time. They are noisy, aggressive and numerous, born opportunists who can make the most of any environment. Starlings are at home in forest interiors or industrial estates and, for many people, they are the scourge of the bird-table. Starlings are gregarious birds that form feeding parties of dozens, and sometimes hundreds, of individuals. When such a group descends on a bird-table it will be completely stripped in seconds.

But the starlings' sociable behaviour is at its most impressive in the evening. They like to roost in large flocks of up to ten thousand birds. When they fly towards a chosen site, the sky can go black for a few seconds as the flock passes over.

In winter they prefer to roost in towns, where the air temperature is slightly higher than the countryside around. Starlings are intelligent birds that are quick to find an uninsulated roof on a heated building. The warmth coming from beneath can make a difference of several degrees and helps keep the birds alive during frosty nights. The Shropshire population of starlings is boosted in winter by birds from Scandinavia. These northern starlings are slightly larger and heavier than native birds, even though they are the same species.

During the summer starlings roost in more natural habitats and frequently choose reed-beds, because the water and mud around prevent nocturnal hunters, like foxes, stalking them under the cover of darkness. The settling basins at the Sugar Beet Factory at Allscott and the smaller pools around Ellesmere are major starling roosts in summer.

Greenfinch

The greenfinch was once a popular cage bird in Shropshire, where it was known as the green linnet. The birds were originally confined to the edge of woodlands, where they were free to feed both in open ground

and deeper in the forest. Today they are most likely to be seen in well-established mature gardens, a habitat very similar to the one in which they evolved. Greenfinches live throughout the county but avoid areas with no trees, this includes wind-blown hills and the busiest part of town centres. Leafy suburbia suits them perfectly.

Greenfinches have strong, solid beaks which are the hallmark of a seed-eating species; they are very fond of corn but are also extremely partial to yew berries. While most finches are shy and wary, greenfinches are quite happy living alongside humans and have benefited enormously from bird tables. Because they are regularly seen around houses, it is tempting to think that greenfinches are very common. But this is a classic error in wildlife recording. The Shropshire population of greenfinches is somewhere around ten thousand pairs while the wren, a bird that is not so reliant on gardens, numbers around a hundred thousand pairs.

Away from parks and gardens, greenfinches are at the mercy of farming practice; when grain crops are ripe and standing, the birds do very well. But after harvesting, the bulk of their food disappears. This constant fluctuation has disastrous effects on the birds. They may produce large broods of young in the summer in response to the massive food supply found in arable fields, but once the chicks have become independent in the summer, the crops may be collected and the birds are left with little to eat.

Blackbird

This bird was once called the 'ouzle' or 'uzzle' in all known written references but, eventually, its more popular and descriptive nickname of blackbird was adopted. And, yes, the nursery rhyme telling of "four and twenty blackbirds baked in a pie" is a true story. For very special occasions empty pastry cases were first baked blind and, when cool, were then filled with live blackbirds. The birds were released when the pie was cut open, marking the highlight of a grand banquet.

Blackbirds were once exclusively creatures of the forest edge and early records emphasised their painfully shy nature. Today the best place to find blackbirds is alongside humans, in parks and gardens. Closely cropped grass, in the form of lawns, is ideal for the blackbird's hunting technique of hop-listen-hop-listen before pouncing on a worm. In autumn, they industriously pick up fallen leaves and flick them away, looking for the worms that are frequently found under damp leaf litter.

The blackbirds' adaptation to an ever growing suburban habitat has resulted in a massive increase in their population. Today there are around four hundred thousand blackbirds in Shropshire making them our most numerous and successful bird. The fact that there are so many blackbirds has, perhaps, made us blasé towards them. For many ornithologists blackbirds rival nightingales as the producer of Britain's most beautiful bird song.

Shropshire has a large number of so-called pied blackbirds, which show obvious patches of white plumage. Birds sporting a single white feather on a wing or tail are often seen. Sometimes from the neck upwards a blackbird's head may be an odd pale-grey colour and occasionally, although still not rare, the whole bird is pure white. This colour mutation is controlled by genes and it so happens that the genetic material of Shropshire blackbirds makes them unusually prone to two-coloured plumage.

Photographic Notes

The photographs were accumulated over eighteen years and were taken on a succession of different cameras, both 35mm and 6cm square format. My current cameras are Pentax and Bronica, used mainly with lenses ranging from 12mm to 300mm. Only one picture, the redshank, was taken on a very long telephoto lens. It is much better to spend time getting close to the animals, as short lenses provide greater flexibility.

A horribly heavy tripod was used for every single photograph, they may be awkward to carry but good tripods really do make pictures sharper.

The filmstock is a mixture of Kodachrome 64 and Fujichrome Velvia.

The high speed photographs were achieved with custom-made flash equipment that gives an exposure of 1/20,000th of a second, at f22 at 1 metre on 50 ISO film. To capture rapid action at the exact moment, the camera is fired by an infra-red trigger that allows the subject to take its own photograph as it breaks an invisible beam connected to the motor drive. The trigger must be positioned across a known flight path and the camera lens is then focussed on the point where the animal should pass through. It is a very unpredictable technique and the success rate often falls to just 5%.

Bibliography

SHROPSHIRE'S WILD PLACES
Andrew Jenkinson
Scenesetters (1992)

SHROPSHIRE MERES AND MOSSES
Nigel Jones
Shropshire Books (1993)

AN ATLAS OF THE BREEDING
BIRDS OF SHROPSHIRE
Shropshire Ornithological Society (1992)

FAUNA OF SHROPSHIRE
H.E. Forest (1899)

Useful Addresses

SHROPSHIRE BADGER GROUP
P.O. Box 100
Ellesmere
Shropshire

BADGERLINE: 01743 271999

SHROPSHIRE BAT GROUP
c/o Andy McLeish
Flat 1, Leigh Manor
Hope, Nr Minsterley
Shropshire SY5 0EX

SHROPSHIRE MAMMAL RECORDER
Dr John McIntosh
Lawton Cottage
Stanton Lacy
Ludlow
Shropshire SY8 2AL

SHROPSHIRE
ORNITHOLOGICAL
SOCIETY
Geoff Smith
Church Cottage
Leebotwood
Shropshire SY6 6NE

SHROPSHIRE
WILDLIFE TRUST
167 Frankwell
Shrewsbury
Shropshire SY3 8LG

R.S.P.B. LOCAL MEMBERS' GROUP
c/o Geoff Hall
Bank House
Woolston
Shropshire SY6 6QB

Index

More books on Shropshire's wildlife and landscape published by Shropshire Books

Shropshire Meres and Mosses

Nigel Jones £4.99

The Shropshire Severn

Editor: Richard Morriss £14.99

The Farmer Feeds Us All

Paul Stamper £4.95

Shropshire Seasons

Gordon Dickins £14.99

Quiet Mysteries

Gordon Dickins £14.99

For a complete list of Shropshire Books titles please contact:

Shropshire Books,
Column House,
7 London Road,
Shrewsbury,
Shropshire SY2 6NW.
Tel: (01743) 255043